TEENAGERS AND SUBSTANCE ABUSE

by
Margaret C. Jasper

Oceana's Legal Almanac Series:
Law for the Layperson

2003
Oceana Publications, Inc.
Dobbs Ferry, New York

You may order this or any Oceana publication by visiting Oceana's website at http://www.oceanalaw.com or contacting Customer Service at 1.914.693.8100 (domestic or international) or 1.800.831.0758 (U.S. only).

Library of Congress Control Number: 2003107644

ISBN: 0-379-11374-0

Oceana's Legal Almanac Series: Law for the Layperson

ISSN 1075-7376

Manufactured in the United States of America on acid-free paper.

To My Husband Chris

Your love and support
are my motivation and inspiration

-and-

In memory of my son, Jimmy

Table of Contents

CHAPTER 3:
UNDERAGE DRINKING

CHAPTER 4:
TOBACCO USE

CHAPTER 7:
SUBSTANCE ABUSE AND SEXUAL ACTIVITY

CHAPTER 8:
DRUG TESTING IN SCHOOLS

APPENDICES

ABOUT THE AUTHOR

MARGARET C. JASPER is an attorney engaged in the general practice of law in South Salem, New York, concentrating in the areas of personal injury and entertainment law. Ms. Jasper holds a Juris Doctor degree from Pace University School of Law, White Plains, New York, is a member of the New York and Connecticut bars, and is certified to practice before the United States District Courts for the Southern and Eastern Districts of New York, the United States Court of Appeals for the Second Circuit, and the United States Supreme Court.

Ms. Jasper has been appointed to the panel of arbitrators of the American Arbitration Association and the law guardian panel for the Family Court of the State of New York, is a member of the Association of Trial Lawyers of America, and is a New York State licensed real estate broker and member of the Westchester County Board of Realtors, operating as Jasper Real Estate, in South Salem, New York. Margaret Jasper maintains a website at http://www.JasperLawOffice.com.

Ms. Jasper is the author and general editor of the following legal almanacs: AIDS Law; The Americans with Disabilities Act; Animal Rights Law; The Law of Attachment and Garnishment; Bankruptcy Law for the Individual Debtor; Individual Bankruptcy and Restructuring; Banks and their Customers; The Law of Buying and Selling; The Law of Capital Punishment; The Law of Child Custody; Commercial Law; Consumer Rights Law; The Law of Contracts; Copyright Law; Credit Cards and the Law; The Law of Debt Collection; Dictionary of Selected Legal Terms; The Law of Dispute Resolution; The Law of Drunk Driving; Education Law; Elder Law; Employee Rights in the Workplace; Employment Discrimination Under Title VII; Environmental Law; Estate Planning; Everyday Legal Forms; Harassment in the Workplace; Health Care and Your Rights. Home Mortgage Law Primer; Hospital Liability Law; Identity Theft and How To Protect Yourself; Insurance Law; International Adoption; The Law of Immigration; Juvenile Justice and Children's Law; Labor Law; Landlord-Tenant Law; The Law of

Libel and Slander; Marriage and Divorce; The Law of Medical Malpractice; Motor Vehicle Law; The Law of No-Fault Insurance; The Law of Obscenity and Pornography; Patent Law; The Law of Personal Injury; Probate Law; The Law of Product Liability; Real Estate Law for the Homeowner and Broker; Religion and the Law; The Right to Die; Law for the Small Business Owner; Social Security Law; Special Education Law; The Law of Speech and the First Amendment; Trademark Law; Victim's Rights Law; The Law of Violence Against Women; Welfare: Your Rights and the Law; and Workers' Compensation Law.

INTRODUCTION

This almanac discusses the social and legal aspects concerning teenagers and substance abuse. Substance abuse is a serious problem among the nation's youth, and contributes largely to the mortality rate of this age group. For example, alcohol use is a factor in approximately half of all deaths from motor vehicle crashes and intentional injuries.

Substance abuse contributes to serious health problems, failure in school, unemployment and criminal behavior. Dependence on alcohol and other drugs is associated with depression, anxiety, and antisocial personality disorder. Drug use contributes directly and indirectly to the HIV epidemic, and long-term alcohol misuse is associated with liver disease, cancer, heart problems and neurological damage.

Destructive behaviors, such as alcohol and drug use, are typically established during the teen years and persist into adulthood. Studies have shown that parental involvement is the single greatest influence on a child's decision to avoid using drugs or alcohol, while peers are the greatest influence on those youths who experiment with drugs or alcohol.

According to a study conducted by the National Center on Addiction and Substance Abuse at Columbia University, the safest teens are those living in two-parent homes who have a positive relationship with both parents, go to both parents equally when they have important decisions to make, have discussed illegal drugs with both parents, and who report that their parents are equally demanding in terms of grades, homework and personal behavior.

Despite all of the campaigns against drugs and alcohol targeted towards the nation's youth, substance abuse among high school and college students is still very high. Approximately one-half of all high school students report using alcohol, with 30% reporting episodic heavy drinking. Marijuana use has increased from 14.7% in 1991 to 24% in 2001. The use of steroids is prevalent among high school and college athletes, and club drugs, such as Ecstasy have become increasingly popular among teenagers. There has also been a disturbing emergence of so-called "date-rape" drugs.

Another area of concern is tobacco use among teens, including cigarette smoking, cigar smoking, and smokeless tobacco use. Tobacco is the single leading preventable cause of death in the United States, causing more than 400,000 premature deaths each year. Approximately 80% of tobacco use occurs for the first time among young people less than 18 years of age. In 2001, 29% of high schools students reported smoking cigarettes, and 15% reported cigar use. In addition, 8% of high school students and 19% of white male high school students reported using smokeless tobacco.

This almanac discusses the scope of the substance abuse problem among teenagers, and the types of drugs most commonly used by this age group. Collaborative efforts and strategies devised by schools, and private and public entities to stop illegal drug and alcohol use are also examined. The government's crackdown on the use of the internet to facilitate the production, use, and sale of "club drugs" is also discussed, and the serious problem of "date rape," and the drugs used to facilitate this crime is also explored in this almanac.

The Appendix provides resource directories, and other pertinent information and data. The Glossary contains definitions of many of the terms used throughout the almanac.

CHAPTER 1:
OVERVIEW OF THE SUBSTANCE ABUSE
PROBLEM AMONG TEENAGERS

IN GENERAL

It is a fact that the United States has the highest percentage of teenage drug and alcohol use of any industrialized nation. Drug and alcohol abuse among young people today presents a very serious problem. In 1999, a study by the National League of Cities cited use of illegal drugs, alcohol, and tobacco among youth as one of the top threats to America in the new millennium.

Unfortunately, teenagers are particularly vulnerable to drug abuse, and their immature physical and psychological development makes them highly susceptible to the negative effects of drugs. Further, behavior patterns that result from teen and preteen drug use often produce tragic consequences. Approximately one-half of all homicides, suicides, and fatal accidents, are reportedly associated with drug or alcohol use.

Studies have also shown that drug use and crime are linked, and account for the increasing number of children who engage in criminal behavior, such as robbery, prostitution and drug dealing, to support their drug habits.

STATISTICS

Drug Use

According to the National Household Survey on Drug Abuse, 10.8 percent of youths age 12 to 17 reported current use of illicit drugs in 2001, which was an increase from 9.7% in 2000. Among this age group in 2001, the percent using illicit drugs in the past 30 days prior to the interview was higher for boys (11.4%) than for girls (10.2%). Marijuana was the major illicit drug used for this age group, with 8% of youths being current users.

According to the Substance Abuse and Mental Health Services Administration (SAMHSA), in 2000, over 3 million youths aged 12 to 17 had used marijuana at least once during the past year, and more than 2 million youths in this age group reported using inhalants at least once in their lifetime. In addition, 23 percent of the 4.5 million people age 12 and older who need drug treatment are teenagers.

According to the Centers for Disease Control and Prevention (CDC) 2001 Youth Risk Behavior Surveillance System (YRBSS), 42.4% of high school students surveyed nationwide used marijuana during their lifetime. Overall, male students (46.5%) were significantly more likely than female students (38.4%) to report lifetime marijuana use.

The YRBSS also reports that 9.4% of students had used a form of cocaine during their lifetime, and 14.7% of students had sniffed glue, breathed the contents of aerosol spray cans, or inhaled paints or spray to get high during their lifetime. Overall, male students (3.8%) were significantly more likely than female students (2.5%) to report lifetime heroin use, and 9.8% of students had used methamphetamine during their lifetime.

According to the Monitoring the Future Survey, in 2002, past month use of any illicit drug was highest for twelfth graders (25.4%), followed by tenth graders (20.8%), and was lowest among eighth graders (10.4%). Twelfth graders, on average, had a higher percentages of use on all drugs when compared to eighth and tenth grades. In 2002, lifetime prevalence of use of illicit drugs for eighth, tenth, and twelfth graders was 24.5%, 44.6%, and 53.0%, respectively.

The large number of eighth grade students who have already reportedly begun use of the so-called "gateway drugs"—tobacco, alcohol, inhalants, and marijuana—suggests that a substantial number of eighth-grade students are already at risk of proceeding further to such drugs as LSD, cocaine, amphetamines, and heroin.

Alcohol Use

According to the SAMHSA survey, in 2000, about 10.1 million young people aged 12 to 20 had used alcohol in the past month. Another study reports that by eighth grade, 47% of youths have tried alcohol, and 21.3% say they have already been drunk at least once.

Nearly 3 million were dependent on or had abused alcohol in the prior year, but only about 400,000 received any type of alcohol treatment. In 2000, almost 7 million young people aged 12 to 20 were reportedly binge drinkers. In addition, underage persons who reported binge drinking were 7 times more likely to have used illicit drugs than underage persons who did not binge drink.

Further, nearly 3 million persons aged 16 to 20 were estimated to have driven under the influence of alcohol at least once in the prior year.

Tobacco Use

Over 1 million children start smoking every year. Of that number, approximately one-half will become addicted. At least 4.5 million American adolescents aged 12-17 currently smoke cigarettes. According to one survey, about one third of eighth graders (31.4%) have tried cigarettes.

SUBSTANCE ABUSE PREVENTION

Research shows that teenagers who do not use drugs are much less likely to start using them when they are older. Therefore, it is crucial that there be a concerted effort to prevent young people from experimenting with alcohol and illegal drugs. Individual substance abuse prevention efforts are designed to shape a teenager's understanding of the dangers of using drugs, as well as teach them skills that help them to stay clear of drug use.

It is important to be aware of both the risk factors and the protective factors that influence whether a teenager will engage in substance abuse.

Risk Factors

A risk factor is a condition that increases the likelihood that a child will use drugs. Studies have shown that the more risk factors a child is exposed to, the more likely the child will fall victim to substance abuse. Risk factors include biological, psychological, behavioral, and social/environmental characteristics, such as depression or antisocial personality disorder, a family history of substance use, or residence in a neighborhood where substance use is tolerated and drugs are readily available.

Protective Factors

A protective factor is an influence that inhibits or reduces the probability that a child will use drugs. Protective factors balance the negative impact of risk factors. Parental involvement is an example of a protective factor. Studies have shown that drug, alcohol and tobacco use is lower among youths who believed their parents would strongly disapprove of their substance use compared with those who felt their parents somewhat disapproved or those who thought their parents would neither approve nor disapprove. Substance abuse prevention programs seek to build up a child's protective factors in order to decrease the child's likelihood of substance abuse.

Environmental Strategies

Environmental strategies are tactics intended to reduce or eliminate substance use among teenagers by making changes in the "environment" in which tobacco, alcohol and illicit drugs are used. Environmental strategies which tobacco, alcohol and illicit drugs are used. Environmental strategies include legislation to control the availability of these substances to youths. Unlike substance abuse prevention programs which are geared towards educating the individual about the harmful effects of drugs, environmental strategies seek to control societal factors that may contribute to substance abuse.

Environmental strategies offer a number of advantages. They reach a broader population. Implementation of regulations afford immediate and long-lasting protection. Also, in many instances, they are more cost effective than individual treatment, which can be undermined by negative environmental factors.

Examples of environmental strategies include:

1. Enacting laws that raise the minimum drinking age;

2. Using alcohol excise taxes to raise the price of alcohol, thus reducing its economic availability to youth;

3. Restricting the physical availability of alcohol by limiting the number and hours of alcohol vendors in a community;

4. Increasing sanctions against drinking and driving by passing stricter laws about blood alcohol content, including "zero tolerance laws" directed at youth;

5. Creating laws and regulations to prohibit retail sales of tobacco to youth;

6. Increasing tobacco taxes to alter the economic availability of tobacco products for youth;

7. Creating "tobacco-free" environments in communities;

8. Setting up surveillance programs so that drug dealing is more visible;

9. Creating zoning and public nuisance laws to force landlords to clean up drug dealing areas;

10. Creating drug-free school zones;

11. Implementing curfews to keep youth off the streets at night, to reduce exposure to illicit drugs, violence and crime; and

12. Mass media campaigns designed to promote drug-free lifestyles.

Enforcement Efforts

Obviously, in order for the environmental strategies to succeed, law enforcement officials must demand compliance with the regulations and policies implemented to address the substance abuse problem. For example, law enforcement officials must vigorously enforce minimum age purchase laws for alcohol and tobacco through compliance checks.

WARNING SIGNS OF SUBSTANCE ABUSE

According to the National Center on Addiction and Substance Abuse at Columbia University, parents should be alert to the following behaviors which may indicate that their child is drinking or using illegal drugs:

1. Low grades or poor school performance;

2. Withdrawal, isolation, depression or fatigue;

3. Aggressive rebellious behavior;

4. Truancy;

5. Excessive influence by peers or change in friends;

6. Hostility and lack of cooperativeness;

7. Deteriorating relationships with family;

8. Loss of interest in appearance and personal hygiene;

9. Loss of interest in hobbies and sports;

10. Changes in sleeping and eating habits;

11. Evidence of drugs and paraphernalia; and

12. Physical changes such as (i) red eyes; (ii) runny nose; (iii) frequent sore throats; (iv) rapid weight loss; (v) bruises from falls.

CONSEQUENCES

A major problem in preventing drug and alcohol use by young people is their inability to appreciate the consequences of substance abuse. For example, youths who did not perceive a great risk in smoking marijuana had higher rates of substance use and were more likely to use illegal substances. Research suggests that young people who perceive greater legal, social, health, family, or personal risk in using drugs are less likely to begin using drugs.

In fact, substance abuse presents an enormous problem to society as well as the user. Studies have shown that, in addition to the serious health risks posed by substance abuse, teenagers using drugs do not perform as well in school as those teens who do not use drugs. In fact, one study found that youths who received grades of D or below were more likely than those with higher grades to have used drugs or alcohol.

Additionally, there are consequences for family members, the community, and the entire society. Crime, domestic violence, accidents, illness, and unemployment can all be linked to illegal drug use. Persistent substance abuse by teenagers often leads to involvement with the juvenile justice system. In addition, illegal drugs are a serious drain on the American economy, accounting for an estimated $110 billion in expenses and lost revenue, including the cost of increased law enforcement, incarceration, treatment, public health costs, etc.

HEALTH RISKS

Illegal drug use is responsible for the deaths of thousands of Americans annually, many of whom are teenagers. In 1997, there were 15,973 drug-induced deaths in America, primarily due to overdose. This number rises significantly when other drug-related causes of death are factored into the total, such as deaths from drug-related HIV/AIDS, tuberculosis, hepatitis B, hepatitis non-A/non-B, endocarditis, motor vehicle accidents, suicide, and homicide, etc.

Studies have shown that long-lasting and often irreversible physical changes take place in the brain following drug use. Because the brain is still developing during teenage years, the adverse effects of drug use on the adolescent brain are quite serious. Drug use can cause overdose, addiction, organ damage, memory problems and death. Drug use can cause serious learning problems, including difficulty in thinking and problem solving, and long-lasting damage to the areas of the brain critical for thought and memory.

Further, studies have shown that youths who reported drug or alcohol use were more likely than youths who did not use these substances to be at risk for suicide. Mental health problems, including depression, developmental lags, apathy, withdrawal, and other psychosocial dysfunctions, are frequently linked to substance abuse among adolescents.

The Drug Abuse Warning Network (DAWN) study reports the number of people seeking emergency department (ED) treatment related to illegal drug use or non-medical use of legal drugs. According to this study, from 1999 to 2001, the total drug-related ED episodes increased 17.1 percent for patients age 12 to 17, from 52,685 to 61,695. Of the 61,695 episodes in 2001, marijuana was mentioned 16,516 times; cocaine was mentioned 3,509 times; methamphetamine was mentioned 1,253 times; and heroin was mentioned 834 times. From January to June 2002, there were 29,846 ED drug episodes for patients age 12 to 17.

SUBSTANCE ABUSE TREATMENT

Treating teenagers for substance abuse can be complicated. Treatment programs must consider the child's age, level of maturity, and family and peer environment. In addition, the usual factors that also must be considered include the severity of the substance use, cultural background, and presence of coexisting disorders.

Admissions for children age 12 to 17 to treatment facilities in the United States increased 38 percent between 1992, when there were 95,000 admissions, and 2000, when there were 131,176 admissions. Marijuana admissions grew from 23% in 1992 to 62% during 2000.

Although seventy-one percent of adolescent admissions were male, this figure was heavily influenced by marijuana admissions, where 76% were male. The male to female ratio was closer for other substances.

About one-half (51%) of adolescent admissions to treatment programs in 2000 were referred by the criminal justice system. Seventeen percent were self or individual referrals, and 11 percent were referred through schools.

Selecting an Alcohol and Drug Treatment Facility

Selecting a proper treatment facility for a child who needs rehabilitation is important to a successful recovery. All aspects of the treatment programs offered should be carefully considered. According to The U.S. Department of Health and Human Services, Substance Abuse and Mental Health Services Administration (SAMHSA), the following 12 questions should be considered when selecting an alcohol or drug treatment program:

1. Does the program accept your insurance? If not, will they work with you on a payment plan or find other means of support for you?

2. Is the program run by state-accredited, licensed and/or trained professionals?

3. Is the facility clean, organized and well-run?

4. Does the program encompass the full range of needs of the individual (medical: including infectious diseases; psychological: including co-occurring mental illness; social; vocational; legal; etc.)?

5. Does the treatment program also address sexual orientation and physical disabilities as well as provide age, gender and culturally appropriate treatment services?

6. Is long-term aftercare support and/or guidance encouraged, provided and maintained?

7. Is there ongoing assessment of an individual's treatment plan to ensure it meets changing needs?

8. Does the program employ strategies to engage and keep individuals in longer-term treatment, increasing the likelihood of success?

9. Does the program offer counseling (individual or group) and other behavioral therapies to enhance the individual's ability to function in the family/community?

10. Does the program offer medication as part of the treatment regimen, if appropriate?

11. Is there ongoing monitoring of possible relapse to help guide patients back to abstinence?

12. Are services or referrals offered to family members to ensure they understand addiction and the recovery process to help them support the recovering individual?

SAMHSA provides a toll-free, 24-hour treatment referral service to help locate treatment options. For a referral to a treatment center or support group in your area, call SAMHSA at 1-800-487-4889 or visit their internet website at http://findtreatment.samhsa.gov/.

A state substance abuse resource directory is set forth at Appendix 1.

SUBSTANCE ABUSE AND CRIMINAL BEHAVIOR

Juvenile Delinquency

Substance abuse among teenagers has been strongly linked to delinquency. Arrest, adjudication, and intervention by the juvenile justice system are eventual consequences for many youths engaged in alcohol and other drug use. Although substance abuse does not directly cause delinquent behavior, and delinquency does not directly cause alcohol and other drug use, the two behaviors are strongly correlated and often bring about school and family problems, involvement with negative peer groups, a lack of neighborhood social controls, and physical or sexual abuse.

According to the Federal Bureau of Investigation (FBI), there were 139,238 juveniles, under the age of 18, arrested for drug abuse violations in 2001. The Arrestee Drug Abuse Monitoring (ADAM) Program tests arrestees in selected cities for drug use at the time of arrest. According to the 1999 ADAM Report, marijuana was the most commonly used drug for both juvenile male and female detainees, followed by cocaine and methamphetamine. Male detainees were more likely to test positive for using an illicit drug than female detainees.

The number of juvenile court cases involving drug offenses more than doubled between 1993 and 1998. During 1998, juvenile courts in the U.S. handled an estimated 192,500 delinquency cases in which a drug offense was the most serious charge.

Drug Trafficking

A major risk factor associated with teenage substance abuse is availability. The so-called "designer drugs," which are popular among teenagers and young adults who frequent clubs, are easily obtainable. In fact, as discussed in Chapter 6, these synthetic drugs, and the chemicals used to manufacture these drugs, along with "recipes" for their production, are readily available over the internet. These chemicals are known as "precursor" chemicals. Marijuana is the only major drug that is a natural product. All of the other substances are manufactured using various chemicals.

These chemicals are purchased from legitimate sources, in large quantities, at low cost. A number of law enforcement initiatives have been undertaken to stop the diversion of chemicals, including various legislative measures. For example, aggressive action by federal law-enforcement agencies continues in order to prevent the diversion of pseudoephedrine cold tablets to methamphetamine manufacturing laboratories.

In addition to this diversion of precursor chemicals to manufacture synthetic drugs, another major problem facing law enforcement is the illegal trafficking of controlled substances, such as pharmaceuticals, narcotics, depressants, stimulants, and other medications which are manufactured to meet legitimate medical needs, but are being diverted into the illegal drug trade.

Legally controlled substances account for over 30 percent of all reported deaths and injuries associated with drug abuse. In 1999, the United States Customs Service seized 9,275 packages containing prescription drugs, and the number of pills and tablets impounded by the Customs Service totalled 1.9 million. In addition, the DEA made 723 arrests for pharmaceutical diversion during the first three-quarters of the 2000 fiscal year.

CHAPTER 2:
ILLEGAL DRUG USE AMONG TEENAGERS

TYPES OF ILLEGAL DRUGS

Substance abuse among teenagers ranges from the use of the more accepted, legal drugs, such as alcohol and cigarettes, to the use of marijuana, inhalants, hallucinogens, narcotics, and so-called synthetic "club drugs."

The Drug Enforcement Administration (DEA) has scheduled—i.e., classified—drugs according to the Controlled Substances Act (CSA), Title II of the Comprehensive Drug Abuse Prevention and Control Act of 1970, as follows:

Schedule I

1. Drug has a high potential for abuse.

2. Drug has no currently accepted medical use in treatment in the United States.

3. There is a lack of accepted safety for use of the drug under medical supervision.

Schedule II

1. Drug has a high potential for abuse.

2. Drug has a currently accepted medical use in treatment in the United States or a currently accepted medical use with severe restrictions.

3. Abuse of the drug may lead to severe psychological or physical dependence.

Schedule III

1. Drug has a potential for abuse less than the drugs in Schedules I and II.

2. Drug has a currently accepted medical use in treatment in the United States.

3. Abuse of the drug may lead to moderate or low physical dependence or high psychological dependence.

Schedule IV

1. Drug has a low potential for abuse relative to the drugs or other substances in Schedule III.

2. Drug has a currently accepted medical use in treatment in the United States.

3. Abuse of the drug may lead to limited physical dependence or psychological dependence relative to the drugs or other substances in Schedule III.

Schedule V

1. Drug has a low potential for abuse relative to the drugs or other substances in Schedule IV.

2. Drug has a currently accepted medical use in treatment in the United States.

3. Abuse of the drug may lead to limited physical dependence or psychological dependence relative to the drugs or other substances in Schedule IV.

A table setting forth the description, use and effect of the most frequently used drugs is set forth at Appendix 2.

MARIJUANA

Marijuana is the most frequently used illegal drug in the United States. Approximately 33 percent (72 million) of all Americans have tried marijuana at least once in their lifetime. During the 1980's, the use of marijuana declined. However, since the early 1990's, the use of marijuana among teenagers and young adults has risen.

There is concern over this increase in marijuana use, particularly because marijuana is viewed as a "gateway" drug, i.e., an introduction to other drugs. In fact, studies have found that nearly all adolescents who use illegal drugs other than marijuana also used marijuana.

Marijuana is derived from the leaves of the Indian hemp plant. The leaves are dried, chopped, rolled into cigarette form or placed in a pipe, and smoked. Marijuana enters the bloodstream and affects the brain and nervous system, causing a variety of effects, including reduced coordination and reflexes, and distorted thinking. Frequent marijuana use may be physically and emotionally harmful and is also associated with a host of other social and behavioral problems, including isolation, poor academic performance, violence, and crime.

INHALANTS

The term "inhalants" refers to more than a thousand different household and commercial products that can be intentionally abused by sniffing or "huffing"—i.e., inhaling through one's mouth—for an intoxicating effect. Examples of inhalants include (i) adhesives, such as airplane glue and rubber cement; (ii) aerosols, such as spray paint, hair spray, and air freshener; (iii) cleaning agents, such as spot remover and degreaser; (iv) food products, such as vegetable cooking spray; (v) gases, such as butane and propane; and (vi) solvents and gases, such as nail polish remover, paint thinner, typing correction fluid, lighter fluid, and gasoline.

The availability and low cost of inhalants make them one of the first substances abused by many teenagers. The rate of first use among youths age 12-17 rose from 11.6 per 1,000 in 1990 to 28.1 per 1,000 potential new users in 1998.

Inhalants cause intoxication, loss of coordination, distorted perception and hallucinations. Overuse can lead to convulsions, brain damage and death, even with first-time use.

HALLUCINOGENS

Hallucinogens, such as PCP and LSD, are natural and man-made drugs which can be taken orally or injected. They affect the brain's chemistry, causing distorted thinking, hallucinations, anxiety attacks and suicidal urges.

PCP

PCP (phencyclidine) is commonly referred to on the street as "Angel Dust," "Crystal," "Hog," "Supergrass," "Killer Joints," "Ozone," "Wack," "Embalming Fluid," and "Rocket Fuel." PCP is a clandestinely manufactured hallucinogen. The chemicals required to manufacture the drug are readily available and inexpensive, and the production process is relatively simple and requires very little laboratory equipment.

In its pure form, PCP is a white crystalline powder that is readily dissolved in water or pressed into tablets. PCP is usually sprayed onto a leafy material and smoked, or is used to adulterate commercially manufactured cigarettes.

PCP has been classified by the DEA as a Schedule II drug under the Controlled Substances Act.

LSD

LSD (d-lysergic acid diethylamide) is commonly referred to on the street as "Acid," "Boomers," "Yellow Sunshines," "Cid," "Doses," and "Trips."

LSD is a powerful hallucinogenic primarily manufactured illegally within the United States using commercially produced chemicals such as ergotamine tartrate, lysergic acid, or lysergic acid amide. Pure LSD is a clear or white, odorless crystalline material that is water-soluble. Liquid LSD is mixed with a binding agent and pressed into pills. The LSD being manufactured today is not as potent as the LSD used in the 1960's, thus it does not often lead to the "bad trips" experienced during that time period, making it more popular.

In addition to hallucinations, LSD users may experience panic, confusion, suspicion, and anxiety. Flashbacks can occur even after the user has stopped taking the drug. Most users of LSD voluntarily decrease or stop using it over time, since it does not produce the same compulsive, drug-induced behavior of cocaine and heroin.

LSD has been classified by the DEA as a Schedule I drug under the Controlled Substances Act.

METHAMPHETAMINE

Methamphetamine, commonly referred to on the street as "Speed," "Ice," "Chalk," "Meth," "Crystal," "Crank," "Fire," and "Glass," is a powerfully addictive stimulant that dramatically affects the central nervous system. Methamphetamine is used orally in pill form, or in powdered form by smoking, snorting or injecting, and is quickly metabolized to amphetamine. The injection of methamphetamine can contribute to higher rates of infectious disease, especially hepatitis, HIV, and AIDS.

Some of the effects of methamphetamine use include increased energy and alertness, decreased appetite, convulsions, high body temperature, shaking, stroke, increased heart rate, and cardiac arrhythmia. Methamphetamine use can cause irreversible damage to the brain, producing strokes and convulsions, which can lead to death.

The rate of first use among youths age 12-17 rose significantly from 1990 to 1998, from 2.2 to 7.4 per 1,000 potential new users. However, the 2000 Monitoring The Future study reports slight declines among 8th, 10th, and 12th graders, in annual use of methamphetamine between 1998 and 2000.

Among high school seniors surveyed nationwide in 2002, 3.6% used methamphetamine at least once in the year prior to being surveyed. In 2001, hospital emergency rooms mentioned methamphetamine as a factor for the emergency room visit approximately 14,923 times.

As of 1971, methamphetamine has been classified by the DEA as a Schedule II drug under the Controlled Substances Act.

COCAINE

Cocaine is a narcotic drug which usually comes in the form of a white powder that is sniffed or injected by the user. It is derived from the coca plant. Cocaine is both a local anesthetic and a stimulant causing the user to experience a localized numbing sensation, as well as stimulation of the nervous system. Cocaine is extremely addictive. Overuse can cause hallucinations, nasal cavity ulcers, depression and death.

Because teenagers are still growing and developing, they are more likely than adults to suffer from the serious physiological and psychological damage cocaine causes, and are much more likely to become addicted in a shorter period of time.

In 1999, 0.7% of youths, age 12-17 reported past-month use of cocaine. The 2000 Monitoring the Future study reports that use of cocaine showed a significant decline in 2000 among 12th graders. Specifically, past-year use of any type of cocaine declined from 6.2% in 1999 to 5.0% in 2000.

CRACK

Crack—a purified form of cocaine—is a deadly and destructive narcotic that has become the illegal drug of choice for many of the nation's youth because it is relatively inexpensive and, since it is smoked, it is easy to use. Crack is known to be far more dangerous and addictive than any of its predecessors, including heroin, and has been found to produce psychotic and violent behavior.

In fact, crack is much more dangerous than powdered cocaine. Because it is smoked, crack immediately enters the bloodstream and reaches the brain in less than 10 seconds, while sniffing powdered cocaine can take up to 5 minutes to reach the brain. The speed in which crack reaches the brain can cause immediate death, usually due to a heart attack or stroke, no matter how healthy the user is. Although both drugs are addictive, crack addiction occurs sooner due to its immediate assault on the brain. In fact, some users have reportedly become addicted after smoking crack for the first time.

The National Drug Intelligence Center (NDIC) has reported that the production and availability of crack is directly linked to the availability of cocaine powder, and improvements in the criminal distribution and production of cocaine and crack have increased their availability in suburban and rural communities.

HEROIN

Heroin has not emerged as a drug of choice for most teenagers. According to the Monitoring the Future study, in 1999, past-month use of heroin among youths age 12-17, was only 0.1 percent. Nevertheless, the rate of heroin initiation for youths increased from less than one per 1,000 potential new users during the 1980s to nearly two per 1,000 potential new users between 1996 through 1998. Among the estimated 471,000 persons who used heroin for the first time during 1996 through 1998, one-quarter were under age 18.

According to the 2000 Monitoring The Future study, past-year use among 8th graders peaked in 1995 and 1996 and has declined 21 percent, from 1.4 percent to 1.1 percent in 2000. Past-year use among 10th graders peaked in 1997 and has remained at that level each year through 2000. However, 2000 was the peak year for past-year and past-month use among 12th graders, at 1.5 percent. This number represents an increase of 275 percent from the 10-year low of 0.4 percent in 1991.

CLUB DRUGS

"Club Drugs" is a general term for a number of illicit drugs, primarily synthetic, that teenagers use at dance parties, known as "raves." Club drugs have gained popularity due to the false perception that they are not as harmful, nor as addictive, as mainstream drugs such as heroin. Nevertheless, as further described below, teenagers who ingest these synthetic drugs are at risk of for all types of short-term and long-term health problems, as well as death.

In addition, because club drugs are often produced in unsanitary "laboratories," by often amateur "manufacturers," the quality and potency of these substances can vary significantly, and substitute drugs are sometimes sold instead without the user's knowledge. All of the club drugs have been scheduled by the DEA under the Controlled Substances Act.

The most popular club drugs are described below.

MDMA

MDMA (methylenedioxymethamphetamine), commonly referred to on the street as "Ecstasy," "E," "X," or "Adam," is reportedly the most popular of all club drugs. MDMA is a synthetic, psychoactive substance possessing stimulant and mild hallucinogenic properties. MDMA reduces inhibitions, eliminates anxiety, and produces feelings of empathy for others. In addition to chemical stimulation, the drug reportedly suppresses the need to eat, drink, or sleep, making it particularly attractive to all-night dance club attendees.

MDMA can cause the user's blood pressure and heart rate to increase to dangerous levels, and can lead to heart or kidney failure. It can cause severe hyperthermia from the combination of the drug's stimulant effect with the often hot, crowded atmosphere of a dance party. MDMA users may also suffer from long-term brain injury, particularly to the parts of the brain that are critical to thought and memory.

MDMA use among teenagers is widespread, particularly among white adolescents. The Partnership for a Drug-Free America's Attitude Tracking Survey reports that teen trial use of ecstasy has doubled since 1995, and more teens in the United States have now tried ecstasy than heroin.

Nearly one-third (32%) of teens in 2000 reported they had close friends who used ecstasy, up significantly from 24% in 1998 and 26% in 1999. The 2000 Monitoring The Future study reports that past-year use of ecstasy by 8th graders increased 82%, from 1.7% to 3.1%, between 1999 and 2000; and past-month use increased 75%, from 0.8% to 1.4%.

Past-month use of MDMA by 10th graders increased 44%, from 1.8% to 2.6%, and past-year use by 12th graders increased 46%, from 5.6% to 8.2%.

Among students surveyed nationwide in 2002, approximately 23% of eighth graders, 41% of tenth graders, and 59% of twelfth graders reported that MDMA was "fairly easy" or "very easy" to obtain. In fact, in 2000, the U.S. Drug Enforcement Administration (DEA) seized more than 3 million MDMA tablets, and in 2001, the U.S. Customs Service seized more than 7.2 million tablets.

Among those high school seniors surveyed in 2002, 7.4% used MDMA at least once in the year prior to being surveyed. In 2001, hospital emergency rooms mentioned MDMA as a factor for the emergency room visit approximately 5,542 times.

As of 1988, MDMA has been classified by the DEA as a Schedule I drug under the Controlled Substances Act.

PMA

PMA (paramethoxyamphetamine) is an MDMA "look-alike" drug that is often "substituted" for MDMA without the user's knowledge when the supply of MDMA is not sufficient to meet the demand. However, because PMA appears to have a weaker effect than MDMA, many users accidentally overdose on this drug by taking greater doses in order to mimic the effects of MDMA.

As of 1973, PMA has been classified by the DEA as a Schedule I drug under the Controlled Substances Act.

GHB

GHB (gamma hydroxybutyrate) is commonly referred to on the street as "Liquid Ecstasy," "Scoop," "Easy Lay," "Georgia Home Boy," "Grievous Bodily Harm," "Liquid X," and "Goop." GHB is a central nervous system depressant which was originally sold in health food stores as a releasing agent for growth hormones that would stimulate muscle growth, until it was banned by the Food and Drug Administration.

GHB generates feelings of euphoria and intoxication. Some users also report that it is an aphrodisiac, and is used as a chemical method of counteracting the stimulant effect of MDMA. In lower doses, GHB causes drowsiness, dizziness, nausea, and visual disturbances. At higher dosages, unconsciousness, seizures, severe respiratory depression, and coma can occur.

GHB is primarily used in liquid form, is highly soluble, and is often added to alcohol or spring water and passed off as a high-carbohydrate health drink. GHB has been used in the commission of sexual assaults because it renders the victim incapable of resisting, and may cause memory problems that make it difficult to prosecute the sex offender.

Among high school seniors surveyed nationwide in 2002, 1.5% used GHB at least once in the year prior to being surveyed. In 2001, hospital emergency rooms mentioned GHB as a factor for the emergency room visit approximately 3,340 times.

As of 2000, GHB has been classified by the DEA as a Schedule I drug under the Controlled Substances Act.

Rohypnol

Rohypnol (flunitrazepam) is commonly referred to on the street as "Roofies," "Rophies," "Roche," "Forget-me Pill," "Circles," "Mexican Valium," "Rib," "Roach-2," "Roopies," "Rope," "Ropies," "Ruffies," and "Roaches." Rohypnol is most commonly known as a date-rape drug, and is legally sold in Latin America and Europe as a short-term treatment for insomnia. It is very popular among teenagers insofar as it produces an effect similar to intoxication, and cannot be detected in a urinalysis.

One of the significant effects of Rohpynol is anterograde amnesia, a condition in which events that occurred while under the influence of the drug are forgotten, making it an ideal drug to use in date rape situations.

Rohypnol also causes decreased blood pressure, drowsiness, visual disturbances, dizziness, confusion, gastrointestinal disturbances, muscle relaxation, and loss of consciousness.

Among high school seniors surveyed nationwide in 2002, 1.6% used Rohypnol at least once in the year prior to being surveyed.

As of 2000, Rohypnol has been classified by the DEA as a Schedule IV drug under the Controlled Substances Act.

Ketamine

Ketamine, commonly referred to on the street as "K," "Special K," and "Cat Valium," is an animal anesthetic that is generally obtained by diversion of pharmaceuticals or theft from veterinary clinics. When used by humans, Ketamine can cause impaired motor function, high blood pressure, amnesia, seizures, delirium, depression, and long-term memory and cognitive difficulties. Due to its dissociative effect, it is reportedly used as a date-rape drug.

Ketamine liquid can be injected, applied to smokeable material, or consumed in drinks. The powdered form is made by allowing the solvent to evaporate, leaving a white or slightly off-white powder that looks similar to cocaine. The powder can be put into drinks, smoked, or dissolved and then injected.

Among high school seniors surveyed nationwide in 2002, 2.6% used Ketamine at least once in the year prior to being surveyed. In 2001, hospital emergency rooms mentioned ketamine as a factor for the emergency room visit approximately 679 times.

As of 1999, Ketamine has been classified by the DEA as a Schedule III drug under the Controlled Substances Act.

RAVES

Synthetic club drugs are most commonly used at teenage social events known as "raves," and dance clubs. A rave is an all-night dance party, characterized by loud, rapid-tempo "techno" music, light shows, smoke or fog, and pyrotechnics.

Raves were underground parties that originated in Western Europe and England in the early 1990's, and began to show up in most metropolitan areas of the United States shortly thereafter. Now, raves are advertised on the internet, often as safe, alcohol-free environments, and targeted towards teenagers and young adults.

Raves are held either in permanent dance clubs or at temporary venues set up for a single event in abandoned warehouses, open fields, or empty buildings. Raves vary in size, and can range from 30 people in a small club to tens of thousands in a stadium or open field.

Club drugs have become an integral component of the rave culture. Although this was not originally intended, raves have created an atmosphere where the energizing effects of synthetic drugs has become desirable, and thus the sale and use of these drugs has flourished. Many rave clubs even provide cooling centers or cold showers so participants can lower their body temperatures due to the excessive body heat caused by club drugs.

Many young rave-goers wear distinctive clothing and carry paraphernalia commonly associated with club drug use and the rave culture. They wear lightweight clothing due to the overheating caused by all-night dancing accompanied by the effect of club drugs, such as MDMA. They also often wear jewelry made of either plastic beads or pill-shaped sugar candies in order to disguise their drugs, e.g., by stringing MDMA tablets mixed with the candies. Many rave-goers also chew on baby pacifiers or lollipops to offset the effects of involuntary teeth grinding caused by MDMA.

Anti-Rave Initiatives

Regulations and Ordinances

In the late 1990's, initiatives began to be developed to reduce the number of raves being held in an effort to curb the use of dangerous club drugs. Several cities passed ordinances aimed at regulating raves. Cities such as Chicago, Denver, Gainesville, Hartford, Milwaukee, and New York aggressively reduced rave activity through enforcement of juvenile curfews, fire codes, health and safety ordinances, liquor laws, and licensing requirements for large public gatherings. Many communities deterred raves by requiring rave promoters to retain on-site emergency medical services and uniformed police security for large rave events.

Operation Rave Review

The Drug Enforcement Administration (DEA) launched "Operation Rave Review" after studying raves in New Orleans and determining that there was a correlation between rave activity and club drug overdoses resulting in emergency room visits. For example, in a 2-year period, 52 raves were held at the New Orleans State Palace Theater, during which time approximately 400 teenagers overdosed and were transported to local emergency rooms.

The DEA, along with the New Orleans Police Department, and U.S. Attorney's Office used 21 U.S.C. § 856 as a basis to investigate rave promoters and to gather evidence that the promoters knowingly and intentionally allowed the distribution and use of numerous controlled substances during rave events. 21 U.S.C. §856 provides as follows:

21 U.S.C. §856—Establishment of Manufacturing Operations

(a) Except as authorized by this subchapter, it shall be unlawful to

(1) Knowingly open or maintain any place for the purpose of manufacturing, distributing, or using any controlled substance.

(2) Manage or control any building, room, or enclosure, either as an owner, lessee, agent, employee, or mortgagee, and knowingly and intentionally rent, lease, or make available for use, with or without compensation, the building, room, or enclosure for the purpose of unlawfully manufacturing, storing, distributing, or using a controlled substance.

(b) Any person who violates subsection (a) of this section shall be sentenced to a term of imprisonment of not more than 20 years or a fine of not more than $500,000, or both, or a fine of $2,000,000 for a person other than an individual.

As a result of this investigation, several rave promoters were arrested and the largest rave operation in New Orleans was closed. In addition, the number of overdoses and emergency room visits caused by club drug use dropped 90 percent, and MDMA overdoses have been eliminated.

The steps used by the DEA and its partners in Operation Rave Review included:

1. Identification of rave promoters, including all parties responsible for managing the production and promotion of the raves, including the owners of the property where the event was held.

2. Compiling emergency medical service (EMS) records of medical transports from the rave venue to local emergency rooms, by court order or subpoena where necessary.

3. Conducting undercover operations inside the venue during rave events, including the purchase of drugs and rave paraphernalia; filming drug purchases and ravers using drugs and rave paraphernalia to enhance the effects; filming the action or inaction of security personnel

hired by the promoter; and filming ravers being treated or transported to hospital emergency rooms.

4. Having undercover agents pose as job applicants for security positions and obtaining information from the promoter during the hiring interview concerning expectations of security when observing drug sales or use.

5. Executing search warrants at the rave venue, at offsite offices, and at the home of the rave promoter, and seizing documents and items relating to the ownership, advertisement, promotion, and operation of the rave venue.

COLLEGE CAMPUS DRUG USE

Illegal drugs have been available on college campuses for many years. Studies show that use of illegal drugs declined in the 1980's but began to rise in the 1990's. The main drug used on college campuses is marijuana, which is seen by some college students as a "recreational" drug that serves as a rite of passage from adolescence into adulthood. According to one survey, in 1997, one out of three college students reported that he or she had smoked pot during the previous year, and about one out of five said he or she had done so in the previous 30 days. The use of ecstasy and other club drugs remains relatively low on college campuses.

A table setting forth annual marijuana usage among college students from 1989 through 2000 is set forth at Appendix 3.

Studies indicate that the combination of alcohol and drugs has led to violence on campus. While students who drink are 1.8 times more likely to experience physical violence than students who don't drink, students who drink and also use marijuana are 3.6 times more likely to experience violence. In addition, students who use additional drugs along with alcohol and marijuana are 4 times more likely as alcohol-only users to report violence.

In cases of sexual violence, students who use alcohol are 2.3 times more likely to report being a victim of unwanted sexual intercourse than those who neither drink nor use drugs. The risk is 4.7 times greater for those who use alcohol and marijuana, and 6.6 times greater for those who use alcohol, marijuana, and another drug.

Many colleges have implemented strategies to enforce anti-alcohol and drug policies.

A sample college alcohol and drug policy is set forth at Appendix 4.

CHAPTER 3:
UNDERAGE DRINKING

HISTORICAL BACKGROUND

Until the late 19th century, there were no minimum age laws regarding the consumption of alcohol. In fact, prior to that time, the frequent use of alcohol was widespread and acceptable for all age groups. Entire families would visit their local taverns, where drinking and fellowship was commonplace. Any problems resulting from alcohol consumption was attributed to the person, and not to the drug.

In the early 1900s, the states began enacting laws which prohibited the sale of alcohol to children. However, these laws were not strictly enforced, nor were children prohibited from drinking. As society became more industrialized, and the local tavern became more of a haven for working men where prostitution and gambling were readily available, alcohol took on a different image. Alcohol abuse was seen as the cause for growing immorality, crime, and violence. A movement to completely prohibit the use of alcohol took hold and was in large part responsible for passage of the 18th constitutional amendment and the Volstead Act in 1919, which made alcohol illegal.

Federal prohibition of alcohol was unsuccessful. It was impossible to enforce adequately and resulted in illegal liquor production and distribution. As a result, in 1933, the 21st constitutional amendment was passed which repealed prohibition, and alcohol once again became legal. Nevertheless, concern over the effects of alcohol continued to be an issue, and strict minimum age drinking laws—usually set at age 21—were enacted by all of the states.

During the Vietnam War, large numbers of young men were drafted at the age of 18, and in 1971, the 26th constitutional amendment lowered the federal voting age to 18. It thus struck many as ironic that a child was considered old enough to go to war and to vote, but was not permitted to drink a beer. In response, the minimum drinking age was lowered in many states.

ALCOHOLISM AND ALCOHOL ABUSE DEFINED

Alcoholism, also known as alcohol dependence, is a disease that includes the following four symptoms:

1. Craving—A strong need, or urge, to drink, which can be as strong as the need for food or water.;

2. Loss of control—Not being able to stop drinking once drinking has begun;

3. Physical dependence—Withdrawal symptoms, such as nausea, sweating, shakiness, and anxiety after stopping drinking; and

4. Tolerance—The need to drink greater amounts of alcohol to get "high."

The risk for developing alcoholism is influenced by a person's genes. However, the child of an alcoholic parent will not automatically become an alcoholic, and some people become alcoholics even though it does not run in their family. Researchers are currently working to discover the actual genes that put people at risk for alcoholism. Increased risk factors include one's lifestyle, including their environment, associations, stress factors, and the availability of alcohol.

Although alcoholism can be treated through counseling and the use of certain medication, it cannot be cured. Chronic alcoholism lasts a lifetime. Alcoholics must avoid all alcoholic beverages, even if they haven't been drinking for a long time, in order to avoid a relapse. Some of the medications used to treat alcoholism include drugs to assist the alcoholic through the early withdrawal period, and drugs which help the alcoholic remain sober, e.g. by reducing the craving for alcohol.

A person can abuse alcohol without actually being an alcoholic, if they are not dependent on alcohol. Nevertheless, alcohol abuse can be just as harmful, and can lead to injury and death, and drinking-related health problems.

BLOOD ALCOHOL CONCENTRATION LEVEL

The primary indicator of whether a person has had too much to drink is their blood alcohol concentration (BAC) level. The BAC describes the concentration of alcohol in a person's blood expressed as weight per unit of volume. For example, at 0.10 percent BAC, there is a concentration of 100 mg of alcohol per 100 ml of blood. BAC measurements provide an objective way to identify levels of impairment, because alcohol concentration in the body is directly related to impairment.

Because the rate that alcohol is absorbed into the blood differs from person to person based on such factors as age, weight and gender, the effect that alcohol will have on a particular person varies greatly. Other factors, such as the amount of food in the stomach, also affect alcohol absorption. Therefore, it is difficult to determine exactly how many drinks will result in a heightened BAC.

STATISTICS

Alcohol is the leading drug of abuse by teenagers in the United States. According to some studies, over 90% of teenagers experiment with alcohol at some time.

High School Students

According to a 2002 study of high school students, almost 50% of 12th graders reported drinking alcohol in the 30 days prior to the study; 30% of 12th graders reported being drunk in the prior 30 days; and almost 30% of 12th graders and 22% of 10th graders admitted to binge drinking at least once a month.

In addition, 21% of 8th grade students reported having been drunk at least once in their lives in 2002; 35% of 10th grade students reported drinking alcohol in the past month; and 30% of 12th grade students reported having five or more drinks in a row in the two weeks prior to the survey.

Drinking on College Campuses

Studies indicate that drinking on college campuses among full-time undergraduate students is a very serious problem, in large part attributable to the college environment. In 2001, 18% of college students aged 18 to 22 were heavy drinkers; compared to 12 percent of 18 to 22 year olds who were not attending college.

According to a number of recent studies, including the 2001 Report of the Task Force on College Drinking commissioned by the National Institute on Alcohol Abuse and Alcoholism (NIAAA), college campus drinking has led to very serious consequences:

1. 1,400 college students between the ages of 18 and 24 die each year from alcohol-related unintentional injuries, including motor vehicle crashes;

2. 500,000 college students between the ages of 18 and 24 are unintentionally injured under the influence of alcohol;

3. More than 600,000 college students between the ages of 18 and 24 are assaulted by another student who has been drinking;

4. More than 70,000 college students between the ages of 18 and 24 are victims of alcohol-related sexual assault or date rape;

5. 400,000 college students between the ages of 18 and 24 report having unprotected sex;

6. More than 100,000 college students between the ages of 18 and 24 report having been too intoxicated to know if they consented to having sex;

7. About 25 percent of college students report academic consequences of their drinking including missing class, falling behind, doing poorly on exams or papers, and receiving lower grades overall;

8. More than 150,000 college students develop an alcohol-related health problem;

9. Between 1.2 and 1.5 percent of college students indicate that they tried to commit suicide due to drinking or drug use;

10. 2.1 million college students between the ages of 18 and 24 drove under the influence of alcohol;

11. About 11 percent of college student drinkers report that they have damaged property while under the influence of alcohol;

12. About 5 percent of college students were involved with the police or campus security as a result of their drinking;

13. An estimated 110,000 college students between the ages of 18 and 24 were arrested for an alcohol-related violation, such as public drunkenness or driving under the influence; and

14. 31% of college students met diagnostic criteria for alcohol abuse.

The Task Force suggests the following strategies in combating underage drinking on campus:

1. Training students to change dysfunctional beliefs and thinking about the use of alcohol;

2. Increasing enforcement of minimum age laws;

3. Lowering the number of businesses selling alcohol within one mile of campus; and

4. Eliminating keg parties on campus where underage drinking is prevalent.

Early Use Factor

Studies have also found that children are beginning to drink at a much younger age. Many children first try alcohol somewhere between the ages of 11 and 14, and some children are as young as 9 when they begin experimenting with alcohol.

Research shows that age at first use of alcohol is a clear risk factor:

1. More than 40 percent of individuals who begin drinking before age 13 will develop alcohol abuse or alcohol dependency at some point in their lives.

2. The occurrence of lifetime alcohol abuse and alcoholism is greatest for those youths who begin drinking between the ages of 11 and 14 years.

Recent data from surveys conducted in 2001 and 2002 show that:

1. In 2001, for youths between the ages of 12 and 20 who reported having had any alcohol, the average age of starting use was 14, generally 8th grade level.

2. The proportion of students who began drinking in 8th grade or earlier increased by 33% from 1975 to 2001.

3. In 2002, almost one half of 8th graders had tried alcohol, and by 10th grade, this percentage rose to more than two-thirds.

4. In 2002, about 41 percent of 9th graders said they had drunk alcohol in the past month, which is more than those who said they had smoked cigarettes.

Demographics

Alcohol abuse and alcoholism affects both sexes and is prevalent among all races and nationalities. Almost 14 million people in the United States either abuse alcohol or are alcoholic. The highest rate of usage is among young adults ages 18-29, and more males than females abuse alcohol and are at risk for becoming alcoholics.

CAUSATION

A great deal of research has been done to determine why teenagers are compelled to drink. Teenage alcohol use is largely due to such factors as peer pressure, and the learned behavior of parental alcohol use. If their friends are drinking, they may also want to drink to fit in with the group. At an age when children are most awkward in social situations, alcohol eases the tension.

Nevertheless, according to the Surgeon General, almost one-third of teenagers who drink do so when they are alone, and 40% use alcohol as an escape from their problems. In addition, many children are curious about alcohol and its effects, and may want to imitate others they have seen drink.

In addition, availability plays a big factor in underage drinking. According to the Harvard School of Public Health College Alcohol Study (CAS), there is a strong link between frequent student drinking and a high number of bars and liquor stores within two miles of campuses.

HEALTH RISKS

Studies indicate that underage drinking may cause a number of health problems, including physical damage to the brain; interference with mental and social development; youth depression; interruption of academic progress; an increased chance of risky sexual behavior, fighting, truancy, stealing; compromised health; and unintentional injury and death.

Studies have also shown that much of the violent crime that occurs is committed by individuals who are under the influence of alcohol. Children who drink have been found to exhibit aggressive behavior and engage in a disproportionate number of fights. Almost one-third of teenage murder victims are intoxicated at the time of their death. In addition, twenty percent of teenage suicides are committed while the adolescent is under the influence of alcohol.

COMMUNITY-BASED ALCOHOL PREVENTION PROGRAMS

Community-based alcohol prevention programs have been successful in reducing underage drinking, in large part, by focusing on the following three key objectives:

Reducing the Availability of Alcohol

Older teens and young adults have considerable access to alcohol, as well as the money to purchase alcohol. Although adults often purchase alcohol on the minor's behalf, many youths are able to purchase alcohol directly. Oftentimes, alcohol sellers do not check a minor's identification to verify their age. Community actions might include:

1. Raising the price of alcoholic beverages, e.g. through taxation. Studies show that an increase in the price of alcohol leads to a decrease in consumption.

2. Limit the number of alcohol vendors in the community, e.g. through zoning and use permits. Studies have shown that large numbers of alcohol vendors in an area lead to greater alcohol consumption and

make it more difficult for law enforcement to monitor underage drinking.

3. Make sure that alcohol licensees and their employees are properly trained concerning underage drinking, e.g., in checking identification and spotting false identification, and in minimum age drinking and host liability laws.

Effective Law Enforcement

Strict enforcement of minimum age drinking laws by law enforcement is an effective way of stopping underage drinking. Compliance with laws which require alcohol vendors to check identification should be enforced and there should be immediate consequences for violations. Law enforcement will often send decoys into establishments to make sure these laws are being observed. In addition, adults who purchase alcohol on behalf of minors should be dealt with criminally. These sales are known as "third-party sales," and are illegal in most states.

Setting Examples

Because children are often influenced by the examples set by their families and the adults in their communities, alcohol consumption should not be promoted either within the family or in the community. For example, there should be a focus on removing pro-alcohol advertisements in the community, such as billboards and store promotions.

A directory of State Enforcing the Underage Drinking Laws (EUDL) Program Coordinators is set forth at Appendix 5.

ALCOHOLICS ANONYMOUS

Alcoholics Anonymous is a fellowship of men and women who share their experience, strength and hope with each other that they may solve their common problem and help others to recover from alcoholism. There are no age or education requirements for membership. The only requirement for membership is a desire to stop drinking. There are no dues or fees for A.A. membership. It is estimated that there are more than 100,000 A.A. groups and over 2,000,000 members in 150 countries.

Alcoholics Anonymous has developed a 12 question quiz to help teenagers determine whether they have a drinking problem.

1. Do you drink because you have problems or to relax?

2. Do you drink when you get mad at other people, your friends or parents?

3. Do you prefer to drink alone, rather than with others?

4. Are your grades starting to slip or are you goofing off on your job?

5. Did you ever try to stop drinking or drink less and fail?

6. Have you begun to drink in the morning, before school or work?

7. Do you gulp your drinks?

8. Do you ever have loss of memory due to your drinking?

9. Do you lie about your drinking?

10. Do you ever get into trouble when you're drinking?

11. Do you get drunk when you drink, even when you don't mean to?

12. Do you think it's cool to be able to hold your liquor?

If the answer to any of the foregoing questions is yes, A.A. advises the individual to seek counseling or contact one of their offices for information and assistance.

SOCIAL HOST LIABILITY LAWS

Social host liability laws hold adults liable for providing alcohol to minors who are not their own children. This is particularly so if a child who is intoxicated causes damage, injury or death, or commits a crime.

State social host liability laws generally provide that adults who provide alcohol to underage drinkers, or who knowingly allow underage alcohol use in their home, can face jail time and/or a substantial monetary fine. In addition, if there are injuries or damages resulting from the minor's underage drinking, the adult will be liable for all such costs.

Thus, parents are advised to make sure there is adult supervision for all children who gather in their homes, particularly when there are teenage parties being held in the home. In addition, any alcohol kept in the home should be placed in a locked, secure location. Also, an adult should never purchase alcohol on behalf of a minor or they risk facing criminal and civil penalties.

Most states recognize the right of a parent to serve their own underage children alcoholic beverages in the privacy of their home, however, they are not allowed to provide their children alcohol to be consumed elsewhere, nor are they permitted to serve alcohol to other underage children, even in their own home.

Nevertheless, according to study conducted by the Johnson Institute ("Johnson Report"), when school-age youth are allowed to drink alcohol at home, they are not only more likely to use alcohol and other drugs outside the home, they are more likely to develop serious behavioral and health problems related to their use of alcohol and other drugs. The Johnson Report also indicates that when parents "bargain" with their underage children—i.e., they allow them to drink as long as they promise not to drink and drive—they are more likely to drive after drinking or be in a vehicle driven by someone who has been drinking.

TEENAGE DRINKING AND DRIVING

For a long time, the legal age for purchasing alcohol was 21 years old in most of the United States. Then, in the 1960s and early 1970s, many states lowered their minimum purchasing ages to 18 or 19 years old. According to the Insurance Institute for Highway Safety, the consequences of this action indicated an increase in the number of 15-20 year-olds involved in nighttime fatal crashes.

Although some states raised their legal drinking ages to try to combat this problem, it was found that teenagers would cross state lines to drink legally. As a result, the incidence of fatal automobile accidents across state lines, due to teenage drinking, rose considerably.

In response, a number of states raised their minimum alcohol purchasing ages—in some states back to 21 years old and in other states to 19 or 20. Subsequent research indicated that states which raised their minimum legal alcohol purchasing age experienced a 13 percent reduction in nighttime driver fatal crash involvement involving teenagers.

The National Minimum Drinking Age Act of 1984

In 1984, 23 states had minimum alcohol purchasing ages of 21 years old. Also in 1984, the Commission on Drunken Driving, formed by President Ronald Reagan, announced its recommendation that there be a uniform minimum drinking age set at 21, based on studies which indicated that raising the drinking age would result in fewer teenage road fatalities. Since states set their own minimum drinking ages, the "carrot and the stick" approach—a fund-based method of coercion—had to be used to bring all 50 states into compliance with this recommendation.

In 1984, The National Minimum Drinking Age Act was enacted. The Act required all states to raise their minimum purchase and public possession of alcohol age to 21. States that did not comply faced a reduction in highway funds under the Federal Highway Aid Act. The U.S. Department of Transportation has determined that all states are in compliance with the Act.

The national law specifically requires states to prohibit purchase and public possession of alcoholic beverages. It does not require prohibition of persons under 21 from drinking alcoholic beverages. The term "public posses-sion" is strictly defined and does not apply to possession of alcoholic bev-erages under the following circumstances:

1. An established religious purpose, when accompanied by a parent, spouse, or legal guardian age 21 or older;

2. Medical purposes when prescribed or administered by a licensed physician, pharmacist, dentist, nurse, hospital, or medical institution;

3. In private clubs or establishments; and

4. In the course of lawful employment by a duly licensed manufacturer, wholesaler or retailer.

State Enforcement

Article XXI of the United States Constitution, which repealed prohibition, grants the states the right to regulate alcohol distribution and sale. State laws may differ, however, each allows local communities to regulate youth access to alcohol through local ordinances and law enforcement.

State laws generally address youth-related violations separately. These include:

1. Sale to Minors—Prohibits vendors or any other persons from selling, giving, or otherwise providing alcohol to minors;

2. Purchase by Minors—Prohibits or limits minors from obtaining alco-hol from vendors or other sources.

3. Possession by Minors—Generally prohibits or limits minors from carrying or handling alcohol.

4. Consumption—Prohibits or limits minors' drinking of alcoholic beverages.

5. Misrepresentation of Age—Provides for penalties against minors who present false identification or otherwise represent themselves as being of legal purchase age.

State and local enforcement agencies may use administrative and/or crim-inal penalties against alcohol law violations. Administrative penalties are assessed against vendors through licensing agencies. Administrative pen-alties include fines, license suspensions and revocations. Criminal penal-ties are assessed against vendors or minors through state or local criminal courts. Criminal penalties include fines, jail sentences and diversion programs, such as community service.

Impact on Teenage Drinking and Driving

The National Highway Traffic Safety Administration (NHTSA) estimates that minimum drinking age laws have saved 18,220 lives since 1975. In 1998 alone, they saved 861 lives. These laws have had greater impact over the years as the drinking ages in the states have increased, affecting more drivers age 18 to 20. The number of fatalities was much higher in past years when many states had lower drinking ages. According to the NHTSA, fatal crashes among young drivers declined dramatically as states adopted older purchasing ages.

In fact, even though more than one-third of all deaths for people aged 15 through 20 in 2000 still resulted from motor vehicle crashes, during the period 1982 to 2000, alcohol-related fatalities for youths 15 through 20 decreased by 57 percent. Thus, drinking and driving is no longer the leading cause of death for teenagers.

Since minimum alcohol purchasing age laws have been effective in reducing alcohol-related accidents involving teenagers, many communities are strengthening enforcement of these laws.

Nevertheless, teenage drinking and driving continues to be a serious problem. Alcohol is still readily available to the underage drinker, who does not have the necessary experience to handle either drinking or driving. Young drivers are still at-risk as compared to older drivers. In 1998, 42 percent of 18 to 20-year-old crash fatalities were alcohol-related. This compares to 38.4 percent for the total population.

Almost half of all teenagers who die in automobile accidents are drunk drivers, or are the passengers of a drunk teenage driver. In fact, alcohol-related automobile accidents are the primary cause of death in children between the ages of 15 and 24. In areas where the laws prohibiting drinking and driving are strictly enforced, however, the incidence of fatal automobile accidents is considerably lower.

Although young drivers are less likely than older teenagers and adults to drive after drinking alcohol, their crash risks are substantially higher when they do. This is especially true at low and moderate blood alcohol concentrations (BACs) and is thought to result from teenagers' relative inexperience with both drinking and driving. More 18 year-olds died in low blood alcohol content crashes than any other age.

Zero Tolerance Laws

Zero tolerance laws make it illegal for drivers under the age of 21 to drive with any measurable amount of alcohol in their system, regardless of the BAC limit established for older drivers. The reasoning and justification behind zero tolerance laws is the illegality of persons under the age of 21 to purchase or publicly possess alcohol. If it is illegal for them to purchase or possess alcohol, they certainly should not be permitted to drive after having consumed alcohol.

All 50 states and the District of Columbia now have zero tolerance laws for drivers under age 21, in compliance with the National Highway Systems Designation Act of 1995. Failure to enact zero tolerance laws would have resulted in a state's loss of federal highway funding.

To comply with the Act, states must:

1. Apply zero tolerance laws to all persons age 21 and under;

2. Set a BAC of .02 or less as the illegal per se standard for drivers age 21 and under; and

3. Require license suspension or revocation for violation of zero tolerance laws.

A table of illegal per se BAC levels for young drivers, according to state, is set forth at Appendix 6.

In most states, a young driver is deemed to have given his or her consent to BAC testing. This is known as an "implied consent" provision. Failure to submit to BAC testing generally results in license suspension or revocation.

Selected implied consent provisions of the Uniform Vehicle Code for Drivers Under the Age of 21 are set forth at Appendix 7.

CHAPTER 4:
TOBACCO USE

IN GENERAL

Smoking has been under attack for some time now, and the health-related risks associated with smoking, such as throat and lung cancer, have been widely publicized. This activity has been banned in restaurants and other public places, and in most workplaces, due to the public's concern over the effects of secondhand smoke on people who have decided not to subject themselves to the health risks of smoking.

Most experts and healthcare professionals agree that nicotine is unquestionably the most addictive drug in use today. In fact, most teens who smoke are addicted to nicotine. They may want to quit smoking, but they can't. When they try to quit, they experience nasty withdrawal symptoms. Nevertheless, over 1 million children start smoking every year. Of that number, approximately one-half will become addicted.

Unfortunately, tobacco is one of the easiest illicit substances of abuse for children to obtain. Studies have found that smoking tobacco appears to be linked to the use of alcohol and illegal drugs, and is often the first drug used by children who use alcohol and illegal drugs.

In addition, a 1999 study by The Substance Abuse and Mental Health Services Administration (SAMHSA) indicates that youths age twelve to seventeen that currently smoked cigarettes were 7.3 times more likely to use illegal drugs, and fifteen times more likely to drink heavily than youths that did not smoke.

PREVENTION INITIATIVES

Most smokers start using tobacco before they finish high school. However, if a child stays smoke-free through school, chances are they will probably never smoke. A child is more likely to smoke if his or her parents smoke. In addition, peer pressure, teenage rebellion, curiosity and a desire to feel sophisticated and "grown up" contribute to the decision to start smoking.

To prevent initiation of tobacco use and to help adolescents quit smoking requires a comprehensive approach. This approach should include: (1) increasing tobacco prices; (2) reducing the access and appeal of tobacco products; (3) conducting mass media campaigns and school-based tobacco use prevention programs; (4) increasing provision of smokefree indoor air; (5) regulating tobacco products; (6) decreasing tobacco use by parents, teachers, and influential role models; (7) developing and disseminating effective youth cessation programs; and (8) increasing support and involvement from parents and schools.

THE ROLE OF TOBACCO COMPANIES IN TEENAGE SMOKING

In large part, the tobacco companies have also added to the problem of teenage smoking. Cigarette advertisements are designed to make teens think that smoking is cool and that everybody does it. These misleading ads appear to increase a child's risk of smoking.

There has been much controversy over cigarette advertising that seems to be marketed towards children, such as the use of cartoon character spokespersons. In addition, tobacco companies often sponsor events which draw young people, such as rock concerts, and distribute promotional items, such as T-shirts, designed to appeal to teenagers.

Tobacco companies have been accused of attempting to replace the loss of adult consumers by trying to influence children at their most vulnerable age, thereby ensuring a future generation of smokers. Although companies vigorously deny this charge, it is a fact that half of all adult smokers start by age 13, and 25% start by age 11. Studies have shown that the younger one starts to smoke, the more difficult it is to quit.

Thus, laws have had to be established to make it illegal to provide a minor with cigarettes, and criminal penalties may be assessed against anyone for selling or furnishing cigarettes to a minor. It is illegal in most states for a minor to purchase cigarettes.

STATISTICS

According to recent government studies:

1. The number of adolescents who become daily smokers before the age of 18 years increased by 73 percent from 1988 (708,000) to 1996 (1.226 million), rising from nearly 2,000 to more than 3,000 persons under the age of 18 years who become daily smokers each day.

2. In the 1960s and 1970s, the rate of daily smoking was highest for persons aged 18-25 years. Since the late 1980s, however, the rate of

daily smoking was similar for adolescents aged 12-17 years and young adults aged 18-25 years.

3. Among persons aged 12-17 years, the incidence of first use of cigarettes per 1,000 potential new users has been rising continuously during the 1990s and has been steadily higher than for persons aged 18-25 years since the early 1970s.

4. At least 4.5 million adolescents aged 12-17 years in the United States smoke cigarettes.

5. Young people vastly underestimate the addictiveness of nicotine. Of daily smokers who think that they will not smoke in five years, nearly 75 percent are still smoking five to six years later.

6. Seventy percent of adolescent smokers wish they had never started smoking in the first place.

7. 28.5 percent of high school students currently smoke cigarettes, down from 36.4 percent in 1997 and 34.8 percent in 1999. Current smoking is defined as having smoked on one or more days of the 30 days preceding the survey.

8. If teen smoking prevalence continues to decline at the current rate, the United States could achieve the 2010 national health objective of reducing current smoking rates among high school students to 16 percent.

9. Lifetime cigarette use among high school students is 63.9 percent, down from 70.4 percent in 1999.

10. In 2001, as in previous years, white and Hispanic students were significantly more likely than black students to report current smoking.

11. More than 6,000 persons under the age of 18 years try their first cigarette each day. More than 3,000 persons under the age of 18 years become daily smokers every day.

12. In 1996, more than 1,851 million Americans became daily smokers, of which an estimated 1,226 million (66.2 percent) were under the age of 18 years.

13. In 2001, over 3 million persons aged 12 to 17 had smoked cigarettes during the prior month.

14. Although it is illegal in the United States to sell tobacco to underage youths, in 2001 almost 2 million youths aged 12 to 17 who smoked cigarettes in the prior month purchased them personally during the same time period.

NATIONAL YOUTH TOBACCO SURVEY

In 2000, a number of states participated in a National Youth Tobacco Survey (NYTS) sponsored by the Centers for Disease Control and Prevention. The school-based survey was intended to enhance the capacity of states to design, implement and evaluate comprehensive tobacco control programs.

Included in the survey were students in grades 6 through 12, including both public and private schools. The schools used in the survey were selected proportional to enrollment size, and the classrooms were chosen randomly within the selected schools. All students in the selected classes were eligible for participation in the survey, which requires only one class period to administer.

The survey format was a self-administered questionnaire which was both anonymous and confidential. The school response rate was 90.0%, the student response rate was 93.4%, and the overall response rate was 84.1%. A total of 35,828 students participated in the survey.

Survey Questions

The youth tobacco survey was comprised of a number of state-approved questions designed to gather data on seven topics, as set forth below:

The Prevalence of Tobacco Use Among Young People

1. How many young people use tobacco?

2. How many young people have experimented with tobacco?

3. How many young people smoke on school property?

4. How many young people use smokeless tobacco?

5. How many young people smoke cigarettes?

6. How many young people smoke cigars?

7. How many young people smoke pipes?

8. How many young people smoke bidis?

9. How many young people smoke kreteks (clove cigarettes)?

10. The age at which young people begin tobacco use.

11. The brand of cigarettes usually smoked.

Tobacco-Related Knowledge and Attitudes of Young People

1. The strength of intention to remain non-smokers among young people who never smoked (the "index of susceptibility").

2. What young people perceive to be the social benefits of using tobacco.

3. What young people perceive to be the health risks of using tobacco.

4. The extent of peer pressure on young people to begin tobacco use

The Role of the Media and Advertising in Young People's Use of Tobacco

1. How receptive young people are to tobacco advertising and other activities to promote tobacco use.

2. The awareness and exposure of young people to anti-smoking messages.

The Minor's Access to Tobacco

1. Where minors usually buy cigarettes.

2. How young people usually get their tobacco.

3. Whether sellers require proof-of-age from young tobacco buyers.

4. Whether minors know their state's laws and regulations regarding the sale of tobacco

Tobacco-Related School Curriculum

What young people were taught in school about tobacco.

Environmental Tobacco Smoke (ETS)

1. The extent of young people's exposure to tobacco smoke at home.

2. The extent of young people's exposure to tobacco smoke in automobiles.

3. Young people's perceptions about the harmful effects of ETS.

Cessation of Tobacco Use

1. The short-term likelihood that young tobacco users will quit.

2. The long-term likelihood that young tobacco users will quit.

Survey Results

The following results were obtained from the national survey:

Prevalence

1. 49.5% of students had ever smoked cigarettes (Male = 50.5%, Female = 48.6%);

2. 23.1% currently use any tobacco product (Male = 26.0%, Female = 20.1%);

3. 17.7% currently smoke cigarettes (Male = 17.8%, Female = 17.7%); and

4. 14.5% currently use other tobacco products (Male = 19.9%, Female = 9.1%).

Access and Availability—Current Smokers

1. 9.6% buy cigarettes in a store; and

2. 61.2% who bought cigarettes in a store were not refused purchase because of their age.

Environmental Tobacco Smoke

1. 42.1% live in homes where others smoke;

2. 69.7% are around others who smoke in places outside their home; and

3. 90.8% think smoke from others is harmful to them.

Cessation—Current Smokers

1. 55.8% want to stop smoking; and

2. 58.2% tried to stop smoking during the prior year.

Media and Advertising

1. 88.6% saw anti-smoking media messages in the prior 30 days;

2. 88.0% saw pro-cigarette ads in newspapers or magazines in the prior 30 days; and

3. 21.7% have an object with a cigarette brand logo.

Tobacco-Related School Curriculum

48.6% had discussed in class, during the past year, reasons why people their age smoke.

A Resource Directory of States Publishing Their Youth Tobacco Survey Reports is set forth at Appendix 8.

HEALTH EFFECTS OF UNDERAGE TOBACCO USE

Unfortunately, children do not consider the long-term health effects of smoking, despite media campaigns, warning labels, and school intervention programs. Studies have shown that the younger a person is when they start to smoke, the greater the risk they have of contracting a disease attributable to smoking.

According to SAMHSA, it is estimated that every day more than six thousand people aged eighteen or younger try their first cigarette, and about three thousand people eighteen or younger become daily smokers. If these trends continue, approximately five million individuals now under eighteen will die early from a preventable disease associated with smoking.

The Effects of Smoking on Athletic Performance

Teenagers are often engaged in sporting activities which require a lot of energy and stamina. It is important to note the negative health effects that smoking has on athletic performance:

1. Nicotine in cigarettes, cigars, and spit tobacco is addictive;

2. Nicotine narrows your blood vessels and puts added strain on your heart;

3. Smoking can wreck lungs and reduce oxygen available for muscles used during sports;

4. Smokers suffer shortness of breath almost 3 times more often than nonsmokers;

5. Smokers run slower and can't run as far, affecting overall athletic performance;

6. Cigars and spit tobacco are not safe alternatives to smoking.

INDIAN BIDIS

A new tobacco-related health problem has emerged since the entry of Indian "bidis" into America. Bidis are unfiltered cigarettes packed with tobacco flakes and hand-rolled in tendu, temburni, or other leaves that are secured with a string at one end. Bidis produced for the American market are flavored to taste like chocolate and various fruits or spices, making them more attractive to minors.

Bidis look like marijuana cigarettes, are easy to buy, and are often cheaper than conventional cigarettes. Bidis are generally available at gas stations, liquor stores, ethnic food shops, selected health stores, and through the internet.

Bidis must be puffed more frequently than regular cigarettes. Inhaling a bidi requires great pulmonary effort due to its shape and poor combustibility. Consequently, bidi smokers breathe in greater quantities of tar and other toxins than smokers of regular cigarettes. In addition, bidis contain in excess of three times the amount of nicotine and five times the tar than regular cigarettes.

Bidi smokers have twice the risk of contracting lung cancer compared to people who smoke filtered cigarettes; five times the risk of suffering heart disease; and a considerably greater risk for cancer of the oral cavity, pharynx, larynx, lungs, esophagus, stomach, and liver.

CHAPTER 5:
SUBSTANCE USE AMONG
STUDENT ATHLETES

IN GENERAL

Although physical and mental health are essential to successful athletic performance, many student athletes reportedly use steroids, alcohol, and chewing tobacco at much higher rates than their non-athlete peers. In addition, student athletes have been know to abuse other drugs, including ephedrine, marijuana, psychedelic drugs, diet aids, and cocaine.

THE NATIONAL COLLEGIATE ATHLETIC ASSOCIATION

The National Collegiate Athletic Association (NCAA) is a voluntary association of more than 1,200 institutions, conferences, organizations, and individuals devoted to the administration of college athletics. The organization's aim is to maintain athletics as part of college programs and to ensure that intercollegiate athletic teams and students represent good conduct.

The NCAA Study of Substance Use and Abuse has measured the substance use patterns of NCAA college athletes since 1985 and provides NCAA policymakers with trends in athlete substance use, as well as with insight into reasons for drug use and student athlete attitudes toward drug testing.

In addition, the NCAA sponsors CHAMPS/Life Skills, a comprehensive educational program for college athletes that addresses a number of issues, including alcohol and other substance use. To participate in the CHAMPS/Life Skills Program, colleges must apply to the NCAA. Once enrolled in the program, colleges receive workshop materials, training, and technical assistance from the NCAA.

The NCAA also sponsors Athletic Prevention Programming and Leadership Education (APPLE) conferences for coaches, trainers, students, and health educators, working in conjunction with the University of Virginia's Institute for Substance Abuse Studies.

Educational materials for substance abuse prevention among college athletes are also available from the NCAA. The organization awards grants to support substance abuse prevention programs targeting college athletes.

Following is the contact information for The National Collegiate Athletic Association:

The National Collegiate Athletic Association
700 W. Washington Street
P.O. Box 6222
Indianapolis, IN 46206-6222
Telephone: (317) 917-6222
Website: http://www.ncaa.org

ALCOHOL

According to a national study of alcohol use among college students, athletes have significantly higher rates of heavy drinking than non-athletes. In addition, athletes tend to drink in seasonal cycles—i.e., when they were in their "off-season."

AMPHETAMINES

According to a national study, between 1989 and 2001, student athletes have maintained approximately the same usage rate of amphetamines, at about 3 percent. The sport with the most amphetamine use by men is rifle shooting, at approximately 8 percent. Among female athletes, the most prevalent use was by soccer players, at about 5 percent.

ANABOLIC STEROIDS

Anabolic steroids have been around since the 1950's, primarily used by athletes for the purpose of building muscles and increasing athletic ability. Anabolic steroids—medically known as anabolic-androgenic steroids—are synthetic substances related to the male sex hormones known as androgens.

Anabolic steroids promote growth of skeletal muscle—the "anabolic effect." "Anabolic" refers to muscle-building, and "androgenic" refers to increased masculine characteristics. "Steroids" refers to the class of drugs.

Anabolic steroids are prescription drugs which have been used by physicians to treat conditions such as delayed puberty, impotence, and disorders in which the body produces an abnormally low amount of testosterone. However, doses taken by steroid abusers can be up to 100 times more than the doses used for treating medical conditions.

Anabolic steroids differ from steroidal supplements, such as dehydroepiandrosterone (DHEA) and androstenedione, which can be purchased legally without a prescription. Users of these supplements are led to believe that they have anabolic effects. However, anabolic steroids are not available without a prescription. Abusers of anabolic steroids obtain these drugs through illegal production, diversion from pharmacies, or drug smugglers.

Method of Use

Anabolic steroids are taken orally, injected directly into the muscles, or rubbed into the skin, typically in cycles over a period of weeks or months. Steroid abusers will frequently use two or more types, such as mixing oral and injectable types of the drug along with other drugs. This practice is known as "stacking." Steroid abusers believe that stacking causes the different drugs to interact and produce a greater effect on muscle size than could be obtained by simply increasing the dose of a single drug.

Another practice involves "pyramiding," in which the abuser starts the cycle with low doses of the stacked drugs, then gradually increases the dosage for 6 to 12 weeks, and then slowly decreases the dose during the second half of the cycle. Abusers believe that pyramiding allows the body to adjust to high doses. A second drug-free training cycle often follows the first cycle of pyramiding in order for the body to recuperate.

Neither the benefits of stacking or pyramiding have been scientifically proven to provide any benefits.

Statistics

According to an annual survey on drug abuse among middle and high school students conducted by The National Institute on Drug Abuse (NIDA), there was a significant increase in anabolic steroid abuse among middle schoolers from 1998 to 1999. Although most anabolic steroid users are male, studies have indicated a rapidly increasing use among female adolescents.

The study also reported that 2.7 percent of 8th-graders, 2.7 percent of 10th-graders, and 2.9 percent of 12th-graders reported having taken anabolic steroids at least once in their lives. These figures represent increases since 1991 of approximately 50 percent among 8th and 10th graders and 38 percent among 12th graders.

According to a study undertaken by the Substance Abuse and Mental Health Services Administration (SAMHSA), an increase in the use of steroids among high school athletes highlights the need for the international sports community to educate youth about the dangers of steroids and other performance-enhancing drugs. Among 10th graders, steroid use increased 29 percent between 1999 and 2000, from 1.7 percent to 2.2 percent.

According to a study conducted by the NCAA in 2001, anabolic steroids are not widely used by intercollegiate athletes, with a usage rate of approximately 1 percent. Nevertheless, this is still more than triple the rate by non-athlete students. Anabolic steroid use among college football players dropped from about 10 percent in 1989 to 3 percent in 2001.

However, thére is some difficulty in obtaining accurate data concerning anabolic steroid use due to the fact that many amateur and professional sports organizations, including the International Olympic Committee, have banned their use. Many users are reluctant to report that they used the drug for fear of being disqualified from sports competitions.

Health Risks

Studies have shown that anabolic steroid abuse can cause many health problems. Anabolic steroid abuse has been associated with liver problems, including fatal liver cysts and liver cancer, jaundice, blood clots, cholesterol changes, hypertension, heart attack, stroke, kidney tumors, fluid retention, trembling and severe acne.

Some studies indicate that steroid abuse may also promote aggressive behavior, such as fighting, physical and sexual abuse, armed robbery, and property crimes including burglary and vandalism. Increased mood swings, manic behavior, paranoia, and delusions have also been reported. Cessation of steroid use may lead to depression, fatigue, loss of appetite, insomnia, reduced sex drive, headache, muscle pain, and joint pain.

Use of injectable steroids presents an increased risk of infection, including HIV/AIDS, hepatitis, and bacterial endocarditis, when the needles used to inject the drug are not sterile or are shared among individuals.

Anabolic steroid abuse can also cause gender-specific body changes in males and females. Males may experience irreversible enlarged breasts, reduced sperm production, shrinking of the testicles, impotence, infertility, and increased risk of prostate cancer, difficulty or pain in urinating, and baldness. Female steroid abusers may develop a more masculine body, including decreased body fat and breast size, deepening of the voice, excessive growth of facial and body hair, loss of scalp hair, male-pattern baldness, changes in or cessation of the menstrual cycle, and clitoral enlargement.

Adolescents may also suffer premature termination of the adolescent growth spurt due to premature skeletal maturation and accelerated puberty changes. Thus, steroid abusers risk remaining shorter than they have been if they use anabolic steroids before their adolescent growth spurt has ended.

Unfortunately, teenagers are least likely to heed warnings concerning the health risks of anabolic steroids. According to the NIDA study, the percentage of 12th graders who believed that taking these drugs caused "great risk" to their health actually declined from 68 percent to 62 percent.

A table setting forth anabolic steroid use among students for the year 2000 is set forth at Appendix 9.

CHEWING TOBACCO

Chewing tobacco, which is also referred to as "smokeless" tobacco, is a highly addictive substance. Although it is thought to create less of a health risk than cigarette smoking, chewing tobacco can lead to oral cancer, mouth lesions and gum disease. According to a national study, chewing tobacco is widely used among male college athletes, especially baseball players, e.g., 41 percent of baseball players and 29 percent of football players had used spit tobacco in the previous twelve months.

DIET AIDS

In an effort to appear fit and quickly lose extra weight, student athletes have been known to resort to diet aids, such as diet pills, laxatives and diuretics. However, the abuse of diet aids can lead to serious health problems, including electrolyte imbalance, muscle and bone loss, and injury. Abuse of diet aids are much more common among women athletes than men, and their use appears to be higher in sports typically enjoyed by women athletes, such as gymnastics, dance, and figure skating.

Ephedrine is an herbal diet aid and energy supplement that has gained recent attention for causing health problems, including high blood pressure and an abnormal heartbeat, and has been linked to a number of deaths. Because ephedrine is considered a "natural" supplement, it is not regulated by the Food and Drug Administration (FDA).

According to a national study, 4 percent of student athletes were found to use ephedrine, and women's ice hockey had the highest rate of ephedrine use at 12 percent. Female gymnasts use ephedrine at the rate of approximately 8 percent, and most male ephedrine users are lacrosse players, at a rate of approximately 6 percent.

MARIJUANA

The NCAA study revealed that more than 27 percent of student athletes surveyed in 2001 reported using marijuana at least once during the previous year. The majority of these athletes reported that they started using marijuana prior to coming to college. Specifically, 63.7 percent of users started in high school, while 12.9 percent started during their first year in college and 8.6 percent after their first year in college.

Among student athletes, 60 percent of marijuana users said they use the drug to serve recreational or social purposes and 34 percent said that they use it because it makes them feel good.

By ethnic group, the highest rate of marijuana use was found among Caucasians, a trend also found among college students in general.

Among those not using marijuana, 27 percent said they refrained because they had no desire for the drug's effects, 24 percent refrained because they were concerned about their health, and 13 percent refrained because it was against their religious or moral beliefs.

A table setting forth annual marijuana usage among college athletes from 1985 through 2001 is set forth at Appendix 10.

OTHER DRUGS

The NCAA study also found that approximately 2 percent of student athletes used cocaine during the previous 12 months, which represented a sharp decline from the 5 percent of athletes who used cocaine in 1989. In addition, 4 percent of student athletes reported using psychedelic drugs during the previous year.

THE U.S. DEPARTMENT OF EDUCATION HIGHER EDUCATION CENTER FOR ALCOHOL AND OTHER DRUG PREVENTION

The Higher Education Center for Alcohol and Other Drug Prevention, established by the U.S. Department of Education, provides nationwide support for campus alcohol and other drug prevention efforts. The mission of the Center is to assist institutions of higher education in developing, implementing, and evaluating alcohol and other drug prevention policies and programs that will foster the students' academic and social development and promote campus and community safety.

The Center offers the following services:

1. Training and professional development activities;

2. Technical assistance, including resources, referrals, and consultations;

3. Publication and dissemination of prevention materials; and

4. Assessment, evaluation, and analysis activities.

CHAPTER 6:
DRUG TRAFFICKING AND THE INTERNET

SCOPE OF THE PROBLEM

Use of the internet has rapidly expanded over the past 30 years, particularly among adolescents, who have grown up with computers and access to the "information highway." Minors and young adults have become the largest segment of the U.S. population with internet access. Approximately 85 percent of Americans aged 12-24 use the internet on a regular basis. About 30 million American children under 18 currently use the internet, and by 2005, this number is expected to increase to more than 40 million.

Although the internet affords educational benefits never imagined by previous generations, it is also the source of potentially harmful activities that threaten the nation's youth.

It has been found that drug offenders are now using the internet to promote or facilitate the production, use, and sale of certain "club drugs"—MDMA, GHB and LSD—to adolescents and young adults in the United States. Minors and young adults searching for drugs can easily find suppliers on the internet.

Law enforcement reports indicate that the source of much of these illegal drugs is foreign. In 2000, the New York Police Department arrested a man for selling illegal substances over the internet, including MDMA and GHB. The sources for at least a portion of his drugs were several Chinese pharmaceutical companies.

Many websites promote the drug culture by providing a wide variety of information on drugs and drug paraphernalia. In addition, many websites are being established to cater to the youth party scene, announcing where the next "rave" will take place, a place where illegal drugs are known to be sold and used.

Federal law enforcement agencies, including the Drug Enforcement Administration (DEA) and the National Drug Intelligence Center (NDIC), are presently assessing the nature of this problem and devising methods to stop these harmful activities. However, trying to uncover and address drug activity on the internet is particularly challenging because information can be transmitted so quickly through the internet. The security devices and encryption technology that protects internet users from the theft of their personal information also assists drug offenders in carrying out their illegal activities with relative anonymity.

Generally, the sale of drugs, or the chemicals needed to manufacture the drugs, are arranged in internet chat rooms. "Recipes"—i.e., the ingredients and instructions—for producing these drugs are accessible on the internet, and many young people are becoming adept at producing these drugs. Explanations of equipment or other resources needed to manufacture drugs is readily available.

Detailed information on administering the drugs and their effects may also be found on the internet, as well as information on how and where on-line drug purchases can be made. Disturbingly, the transmission of erroneous information is also common, which can lead to serious injury, illness or death.

The NDIC conducted internet searches in order to assess the availability of drug information to the typical internet user, using conventional on-line search engines such as Yahoo, Google and Alta Vista. NDIC identified 52 sites that contained drug activity information, as follows:

1. 39 sites contained information on MDMA, GHB, or LSD use.

2. 24 sites contained information on MDMA, GHB, or LSD production.

3. 6 sites contained information on MDMA, GHB, or LSD sales.

4. 35 sites contained links to other drug-related sites.

5. 32 sites probably were associated with drug legalization groups.

6. 10 sites were personal websites maintained by individuals.

7. 10 sites probably were associated with businesses.

8. 8 sites probably were associated with "party scene" or rave groups.

9. 20 sites contained a "for information purposes only" disclaimer.

10. 2 sites contained information on how to evade law enforcement efforts.

11. 7 sites targeted young people implicitly or explicitly.

12. 14 sites provided connections to chat rooms or other interactivity tools relating to drug activity.

For further information, the NDIC can be contacted as follows:

National Drug Intelligence Center
8201 Greensboro Drive, Suite 1001
McLean, VA 22102-3840
Tel: 703-556-8970
FAX: 703-556-7807
WEB: http://ndicosa

SOURCES OF INFORMATION

Federal law enforcement authorities have identified the following sources of drug information on the internet:

1. Drug Offenders—Drug Offenders use the Internet to expand their customer base by inducing a young audience to engage in illegal or harmful behavior, such as drug trafficking, credit card fraud and other financial crimes.

2. Drug Culture Advocates—Drug culture advocates are mainly interested in expanding the size of their community to both legitimize their activity and increase pressure on lawmakers to change or abolish drug control laws. They share information on the Internet to demonstrate the ease with which drugs can be produced, trafficked, and obtained. They promote illegal substance abuse by glamorizing drug use.

3. Freedom of Expression Advocates—Freedom of expression advocates publish information on the internet to push the boundaries of self-expression and the First Amendment. Unfortunately, the information they provide may induce minors and young adults to break drug laws or to become a danger to themselves or to others by abusing illegal drugs.

4. Anarchists—Anarchists are individuals or groups who seek to abolish current legal, social, or economic structures, and who are known to disseminate drug information on the internet as a means of advancing their cause by promoting countercultural behavior.

5. Others—Other lawbreakers, including pornographers and pedophiles, use drug websites to encourage young people to perpetrate crimes, or to lure them into being victims of crime.

Most individuals maintaining pro-drug websites provide a disclaimer, which they believe shields them from law enforcement scrutiny. However, such disclaimers are generally viewed as insincere, particularly when the website contains a large amount of information promoting the drug culture and illegal substance abuse.

LOCATING THE THREAT

Trying to pinpoint the location of the drug threat is very complex as the information moves so swiftly across the internet. Three locations have been identified where the source of the information may be found:

1. The Insertion Point—This is the point where the website's creator originates the information and uploads it to the internet, e.g., the author's personal computer system.

2. The Hosting Point—This is the point where the website is stored, or hosted, e.g., the web server of the user's internet service provider.

3. The Receiving Point—This is the point where the end user receives the information, e.g., the end user's personal computer.

Identifying the insertion point and the hosting point can be difficult, because geographical addresses and internet addresses of websites can be hidden through a variety of software or hardware techniques. However, if the website is accessible to all internet users, then the geographical location of the router supporting the website can be pinpointed by tracing the path the information stream follows between its origin and destination points.

This trace will yield the specific location of the router nearest to the web server hosting the website that contains the potentially harmful information. The router's location therefore will indicate the general geographical vicinity of the web server, since routers support servers in designated geographical regions.

Identifying the receiving point would involve more intrusive means of information collection, and even then results may vary according to how the user accesses the Internet.

If a personal computer were used, its location could be ascertained by examining the internet service provider's customer records. However, this would require a subpoena. A Title II wiretap may also be used, however, this would require a court order. Alternatively, a search warrant could be obtained in order to perform a forensic search of the computer's hard drive to find out whether the end user had been the recipient of such information.

Individuals or groups that operate pro-drug websites on their own registered domain name are the most readily identifiable. This is because one must provide personal identifying information about themselves in order to obtain a registered domain name, such as their name, address, phone number, credit card number, etc.. Even if the information given is fictitious, the domain owner may also be tracked down through the payment made for the annual registration of the domain name. Nevertheless, those who operate domain names registered outside the country are not subject to U.S. law.

PRODUCTION, USE AND SALE OF CLUB DRUGS

Of particular concern is the transmission through the internet of information concerning the production, use and sale of MDMA, GHB, and LSD—three significant "club drugs." Because these drugs are classified as Schedule I controlled substances, the sale of these substances is not generally advertised on the internet.

MDMA

MDMA (methylenedioxymethamphetamine), also known as "Ecstasy," and "X," is a Schedule I drug under the Controlled Substances Act (21 U.S.C. § 812), and selling the drug over the internet is prohibited. MDMA is portrayed on the internet as a relatively benign drug with few negative side effects, while at the same time warnings of dehydration and the need for rehydration are also transmitted to potential users.

Although MDMA is generally produced outside the United States, the potential exists for expanded production in the country, and is within the capabilities of many young people who are able to purchase the necessary chemicals.

MDMA is synthesized from several chemicals, most of which are federally controlled. Those wishing to produce MDMA are able to use the internet to obtain the necessary chemicals, recipes and production instructions. In fact, the DEA arrested two chemistry students who used internet instructions to produce MDMA.

The Ecstasy Anti-Proliferation Act of 2000

Due to the extensive misuse of this drug by teenagers, legislation has been passed which significantly stiffens the penalties for the sale of distribution of Ecstasy. The Ecstasy Anti-Proliferation Act of 2000 increases sentences for trafficking 800 ecstasy pills by 300 percent, from 15 months to 5 years. It also increases the penalties for trafficking 8,000 ecstasy pills by almost 200 percent, from 41 months to 10 years.

GHB

GHB—gamma-hydroxybutyrate—was classified as a Schedule I drug under the Controlled Substances Act (21 U.S.C. § 812) on February 18, 2000. GHB is promoted as an athletic performance enhancer, an antidepressant, and a sleep aid. Like MDMA, GHB is also portrayed as a relatively benign

---

drug on many internet websites, along with a warning that it is extremely important to ingest the correct dose. Incidents of addiction, overdose, and death are downplayed.

The use of GHB in drug-facilitated rape is often dismissed as media hype. However, two brothers were recently sentenced to 4 years each for selling GHB "date rape" kits over the internet to customers in New Jersey and other states. They earned approximately $200,000 between March 1999 and January 2000 from these sales.

GHB is more frequently being produced in the United States, particularly since it is supposedly such an easy drug to make. The necessary chemicals are available on the internet, as well as a variety of recipes, however many have been found to contain misinformation.

LSD

LSD—lysergic acid diethylamide—is also a Schedule I controlled substance. Many websites discuss the history of LSD use in the 1960's, and proclaim that the drug has no potential for physical or psychological addiction, although most sites warn that LSD users may experience adverse hallucinogenic experiences. Information about the psychological dangers, flashbacks, and insomnia often associated with LSD use are commonly contained on the website as well.

Although the production of LSD requires the knowledge and skills of a trained chemist, recipes for making LSD are still readily available on the internet. Nevertheless, LSD production instructions on the internet often warn that production should be undertaken by experienced chemists only, and that the necessary chemicals are difficult to obtain.

CONTROLLED SUBSTANCES

The availability of controlled substance advertised as "prescription-free pharmaceuticals" over the Internet represents yet another challenge for law enforcement. Prescription drug seizures by the United States Customs Service jumped from 294 in fiscal year 1998 to 518 in fiscal year 1999.

However, a major roadblock in intercepting these shipments is the manner in which they are shipped. For example, internet pharmacies often ship these substances by way of private express consignment shippers, such as Federal Express and UPS, rather than the United States Postal Service.

During 2001, approximately 8,000 clandestine methamphetamine laboratories and 13 GHB laboratories were seized nationwide.

LEGAL ISSUES

The emergence of the internet as another mechanism for illegal drug trafficking has raised a number of legal issues confronting law enforcement authorities and legislators. Methods developed and laws enacted to combat on-line drug trade must meet constitutional standards and comply with federal statutes.

First Amendment

Government efforts to restrict the dissemination of information concerning the production, distribution and use of illegal drugs must comply with the First Amendment protection of an individual's right to freedom of speech. Thus, the government's right to prohibit an individual from disseminating such information over the internet depends on the type of information disseminated, the manner in which it is disseminated, and the intent with which it is disseminated. The U.S. Supreme Court has ruled that any attempt to prohibit the dissemination of such information would violate First Amendment rights.

Jurisdictional Issues

Because the internet is not confined to geographical boundary lines, law enforcement must determine the location of the criminal activity and the particular jurisdiction's legal requirements. For example, law enforcement is generally unable to do anything about criminal activity conducted over the internet from a foreign country.

In addition, even when the criminal activity is located within the United States, jurisdictional problems may arise where the individuals committing the crime are located in one geographical area while the computers storing the data can be located in an entirely different geographical area.

Evidentiary Issues

In order to use computer records as evidence in court, the government must establish that they are "authentic," and authentication of computer records can be difficult. Computer errors are common, and computer records are easily altered or destroyed. Also, unlike handwriting, the author of computer records is not readily identifiable through analysis.

Privacy Laws

Forensic searches of computers by law enforcement authorities in order to obtain evidence of criminal activity must comply with federal privacy statutes. These include the Privacy Protection Act (PPA), 42 U.S.C. § 2000aa, and the Electronic Communications Privacy Act (ECPA), 18 U.S.C. § 2701, et seq.

The PPA generally prohibits law enforcement officers from seizing materials that are possessed for the purpose of publishing information to the public, and a person using a computer to post information on the internet may be considered a publisher under the PPA. Although an exception exists under the PPA which permits law enforcement officers to seize materials that are evidence of a crime, the officers cannot seize all the data on the computer, and officers may have difficulty separating information that is legally protected from information that is evidence of a crime.

The ECPA protects the privacy of electronic communications, and law enforcement officers must take special precautions when searching or seizing computers that contain electronic communications from third parties.

Both the PPA and the ECPA impose civil liability on law enforcement officers who fail to comply with these statutes.

CHAPTER 7:
SUBSTANCE ABUSE AND SEXUAL ACTIVITY

IN GENERAL

Studies have shown that juvenile drug and alcohol abuse and sexual activity are strongly linked. According to a study undertaken by the National Center on Addiction and Substance Abuse (CASA), increased promiscuity leads to a greater risk for sexually transmitted diseases and unplanned teenage pregnancy. As set forth below, the statistics are alarming.

The study found that adolescents aged fourteen and younger who use alcohol are twice as likely to engage in sexual behaviors than non-drinkers, and drug users are five times more likely to be sexually active than those youths who do not engage in sexual activity. Teens between the ages of fifteen and nineteen who drink are seven times more likely to have sex and twice as likely to have four or more partners than those who refrain from alcohol. The study also found that more than 50 percent of teenagers say that sex while drinking or on drugs often produces unplanned pregnancies.

SEXUAL ASSAULT AND DATE RAPE

Alcohol and drugs are known to be a significant factor in the sexual assault of young women by young men with whom they are acquainted. This is generally referred to as "date rape" or "acquaintance rape," and has become a problem on college campuses. According to the National College Women Sexual Victimization (NCWSV) study, 20–25 percent of college women are victims of an attempted or completed rape, and in 9 out of 10 cases, the offenders are known to the victims. In fact, 12.8 percent of completed rapes, 35.0 percent of attempted rapes, and 22.9 percent of threatened rapes take place during a date. Although a woman's behavior does not cause acquaintance rape, it appears that frequent or excessive drinking is a contributing factor.

Sexual assault and acquaintance rape on campus results from multiple factors, including the offender's misperception of verbal and nonverbal cues, particularly when alcohol and drugs are involved. In fact, most college men who commit acquaintance rape or sexual assault are not even aware that their behavior is offensive or unreasonable.

For example, they may believe it is perfectly acceptable to persuade their date to use alcohol or drugs so that she will be less capable of defending against a sexual advance. However, they would never perceive this as being a scenario involving rape or sexual assault. In addition, because alcohol slows motor functions, reducing the likelihood that a woman can verbally or physically resist an attack, the perpetrator often misinterprets this lack of resistance as consent.

The National Institute on Alcohol Abuse and Alcoholism (NIAAA) estimates that more than 70,000 students between the ages of 18 and 24 survive alcohol-related sexual assault or date rape each year. In addition, a national survey of more than 14,000 students found that 1.0 percent of students living in residence halls or fraternity/sorority houses survived alcohol-related sexual assault or date rape during 2001. This study also found that 19.5 percent of students experienced an unwanted sexual advance where alcohol was involved. Further, a study of students victims of sexual aggression found that 68 percent of the male perpetrators had been drinking at the time of the attack. Research also indicates that in over 75 percent of college rapes, the offender, the victim or both had been drinking.

DATE RAPE DRUGS

There are a variety of drugs that are used to overpower a woman's will, or even cause her to suffer blackouts during which time a sexual assault takes place. These drugs have become known as "date rape drugs." Alcohol is the most commonly used date rape "drug." Other nonalcoholic date rape drugs include marijuana, cocaine, rohypnol, gamma hydroxybutyrate (GHB), benzodiazepines, ketamine, barbiturates, chloral hydrate, methaqualone, heroin, morphine, LSD, and other hallucinogens.

The most incapacitating of the nonalcoholic date rape drugs are rohypnol and GHB.

Rohypnol is also commonly referred to as "roofies," and those who use it appear intoxicated. The effect is almost immediate and lasts for hours. Because this drug metabolizes quickly, it is undetectable in the system within 72 hours after being taken.

Rohypnol can cause amnesia, dizziness, disorientation, confusion, drowsiness, impaired motor skills, impaired judgment, and unconsciousness. When mixed with alcohol, rohypnol can cause dangerously low blood pressure, difficulty breathing, coma and death.

One of the significant effects of Rohypnol is anterograde amnesia, a condition in which events that occurred while under the influence of the drug are forgotten, making it ideal for date rape. This side effect was a large factor in its inclusion in the Drug-Induced Rape Prevention and Punishment Act of 1996.

Gamma hydroxybutyrate (GHB), commonly referred to as "liquid ecstasy," is another frequently used date rape drug. The side effects of GHB include severe memory loss, disorientation, dizziness, drowsiness, nausea, vomiting, breathing difficulty, seizure, unconsciousness, and coma.

Because of the serious side effects of these drugs, and their impact on memory, victims who are given the drugs oftentimes cannot recall whether they were actually sexually assaulted.

On February 18, 2000, Clinton signed the Hillory J. Farias and Samantha Reid Date-Rape Prohibition Act of 2000. This legislation made GHB a Schedule I drug under the CSA.

CHAPTER 8:
DRUG TESTING IN SCHOOLS

GOVERNING LAW

In their 1995 decision in *Vernonia v. Acton*, the United States Supreme Court held that student athletes are subject to drug and alcohol testing because athletic programs are voluntary and student athletes are role models for the student body. In June 2002, the Court expanded the authority of the public schools to perform drug tests on students.

In *Board of Education of Independent School District No. 92 of Pottawatomie County v. Earls*, the Court held that random drug testing on all middle and high school students who participate in competitive extracurricular activities was permissible. Prior to this decision, drug testing was only permitted for student athletes.

ADVANTAGES OF DRUG TESTING

Drug testing can be an effective way to prevent drug use among teenagers. The fear of getting caught through random testing is often enough to deter the average teenager from experimenting with drugs. In addition, it provides those teens who might otherwise fall victim to peer pressure with a very good reason to decline invitations to use drugs.

Drug testing can also alert parents when their teenager already has a drug problem. Early intervention and treatment, if appropriate, can be implemented, averting potentially serious health problems. This is crucial because drug use often leads to addiction and can quickly ruin the teenager's future and destroy his or her family. Students who use drugs or alcohol are more likely to drop out of school, become unemployed, and get involved with violence and criminal activities.

DISADVANTAGES OF DRUG TESTING

Although the advantages of drug testing appears to outweigh any disadvantages, there are risks that school officials should address. For example, drug tests are not always accurate, therefore, a positive finding should always be followed up by a lab test to confirm the original result.

It is also important for school officials to know what types of drugs are prevalent among the students, so they can make sure they use tests that will detect the substances most likely to be used. Unfortunately, there is presently no standard test which can detect inhalant abuse, a common form of substance abuse among teenagers. Inhalant abuse refers to the inhalation or sniffing of certain products such as glue, spray paint gasoline, etc. Inhalant abuse is very serious and can cause severe health problems and death.

PRIVACY RIGHTS

Students have a right to privacy in drug testing, therefore, it is important that school officials protect the confidentiality of any drug test results. The only individuals who are generally entitled to know the results of the tests are the student's parents and certain school administrators, not including the student's teachers.

It should be noted that many students who are faced with substance abuse problems are afraid to seek help voluntarily because they don't want their parents to find out. Many states have recognized that it is better that a teenager get the help they need, even if that means keeping the parents in the dark about the child's drug use. Presently, minors in 45 states and the District of Columbia can consent to treatment for substance abuse without obtaining parental consent or involvement.

TYPES OF DRUG TESTING

Drug testing is used to determine whether an individual has used alcohol or illegal drugs. Certain tests are used to detect specific types of drugs. In addition, some tests can only detect recent drug use, while other tests can demonstrate long-term drug use.

Breathalyzer Test

A breathalyzer test detects and measures an individual's current alcohol levels. The person being tested blows into a breathalyzer machine, which records the results as a number, known as the blood alcohol concentration (BAC). This shows the level of alcohol in the individual's blood at the time the test is taken.

Urine Test

A urinalysis is the most common technique of drug testing used. It is the least expensive method of testing, and has proven to be the most accurate and reliable method. Thus, urine testing is the most likely method of testing to withstand a legal challenge.

Urine tests demonstrate the presence or absence of specific drugs or drug metabolites in the urine. Drug metabolites are drug residues that remain in the system after the physical effects of the drug are no longer apparent. Thus, a positive urine test does not necessarily mean that the individual being tested was under the influence of drugs at the time of the test. The test detects use of a particular drug within the previous few days.

Urine tests can be used to detect the use of alcohol, nicotine, and illegal drugs, including but not limited to marijuana, phencyclidine (PCP), cocaine, amphetamines, ecstasy, and LSD.

Hair Test

A hair analysis is another method of testing that can detect past use of a variety of illegal drugs for as far back as 3 months. The advantages of a hair analysis is that the specimen does not deteriorate, is easy to collect, and more convenient to store because it does not need to be refrigerated. However, hair testing is more expensive than other methods of testing, and will not detect recent drug use—e.g., within 1 to 7 days prior to testing. In addition, hair testing cannot be used to detect alcohol use.

Sweat Patch Test

The sweat patch is a type of drug test which uses a skin patch, worn on the skin, to measure drugs and drug metabolites in the individual's perspiration. The sweat patch is not commonly used for drug testing in schools or in the workplace, and there is presently a limited number of laboratories that are able to process the results.

Oral Fluid Test

A less intrusive method of detecting the presence of drugs, drug metabolites, and alcohol is by testing the saliva collected from the individual's mouth. The most common way of collecting a specimen is by swabbing the inner cheek of the person being tested. This type of testing can determine current use and impairment of the individual, however, because drugs and drug metabolites do not remain in oral fluids as long as they do in urine, a longer history of drug use cannot be detected using this method. In addition, oral fluid testing is less effective than other methods in detecting marijuana use.

IMPLEMENTING A DRUG TESTING PROGRAM

If school officials determine that a drug testing program is needed, careful planning should be undertaken prior to its implementation. The advice of certain professionals should be consulted, including law enforcement officials and drug treatment counselors. Input from the students and parent community should also be sought. In addition, an attorney familiar with student drug testing laws should be asked to review the program to make sure it is constitutionally sound and abides by the applicable law.

In order to be effective, it is important that any drug testing program begin with a clearly written policy which should include the following information:

1. How students will be selected for drug testing;

2. The manner in which drug testing will be undertaken, including the credentials of those who will conduct the testing;

3. Who is responsible for the cost of drug testing;

4. Whether there will be a second confirming test to be performed;

5. The consequences of a positive drug test, including any disciplinary action;

6. How students who test positive will be helped, e.g. counseling, treatment, etc.

7. The consequences of refusing to take the drug test;

8. How students and parents will be informed of the test results;

9. Who will have access to the test results;

10. How the student's privacy will be protected and maintained; and

11. The student's right to appeal the test results and/or any disciplinary action taken.

Costs of Testing

The costs of drug testing in schools are generally paid for through Federal grants from the Substance Abuse and Mental Health Services Administration (SAMHSA) or the U. S. Department of Education's Safe and Drug-Free Schools Program, or through private funding. Although the exact cost varies according to the type of test and the drugs involved, it is generally between $10 and $30 per test. The price for alcohol testing usually ranges from $1 to $10 per test.

Test Administration

In general, a student who is chosen to undergo a drug test meets with a trained test administrator, who collects the specimen to be tested. The test administrator must be careful to keep track of a particular specimen by completing a chain of custody form so that specimens do not get mixed up during handling. Tamper-resistant strips are generally placed over specimen containers to make sure there is no contamination and to ensure that the specimen is readily identifiable. The student is usually asked to initial the specimen container.

If a negative result is obtained, the specimen is discarded. If a positive result is obtained, the specimen will be re-tested in a laboratory for confirmation, and then reviewed by a medical professional to make sure that the test did not detect the use of a legally prescribed drug. In order to ensure the utmost accuracy and reliability, many schools rely on laboratories that are certified by the Substance Abuse and Mental Health Services Administration (SAMHSA).

Disciplinary Measures

Although a positive result on a drug test must result in some disciplinary measures against the student, any effective drug testing program must also recognize the need for intervention in the form of counseling and, if necessary, treatment for the child. Parents must be notified so that they can best decide how to help their child. Teenagers who are occasional drug users may be able to stop using drugs fairly easily once their drug use has been discovered and addressed. More frequent drug users must be evaluated more thoroughly to determine their level of drug dependence, and whether treatment is necessary.

SCHOOL SEARCHES

If a student is suspected of using or distributing drugs in school, the school officials may wish to conduct a search of the student, and his or her belongings. However, the school officials suspicions must be reasonable in order to justify a search.

In their 1985 decision in *New Jersey v. T.L.O.*, the U.S. Supreme Court ruled that school officials may search students without a warrant when they have reasonable grounds for suspecting that the search will turn up evidence that the student has violated the law, or rules of the school. However, school officials may not conduct a search unless they have a good reason to believe that the individual being searched is the one who broke the law or the school rule.

Strip Searches

All searches must be conducted in a reasonable manner, taking into consideration the student's age. Strip searches are illegal in many states. If a state permits strip searching a student, they must be prepared to justify the search based on the severity of the suspected offense.

School Lockers

States are split on the issue of whether school lockers can be legally searched without cause. Some states have found a privacy interest in a student's locker and require school officials to have some reasonable basis to suspect that there is something illegal in the locker before they can search it. Case law has held that the search of student property is permissible where the school officials have a reasonable suspicion that an infraction has occurred and the search is related to that suspicion.

Since lockers are considered school property, school officials generally have the right to search lockers where there is reasonable suspicion. Some states provide that merely because a student locker is considered school property it is searchable and they are not subject to the reasonable suspicion test.

APPENDIX 1:
STATE SUBSTANCE ABUSE
RESOURCE DIRECTORY

STATE DEPARTMENT	ADDRESS	TELEPHONE	FACSIMILE
Alabama Department of Mental Health	100 N. Union Street Montgomery, AL 36130-1410	334-242-3961	334-242-0759
Alaska Department of Health and Social Services	240 Main Street Suite 700 Juneau, AK 99801	907-465-2071	907-465-2185
Arizona Department of Health Services	2122 East Highland Street Suite 100 Phoenix, AZ 85016	602-381-8922	602-553-9143
Arkansas Department of Health, Alcohol and Drug Abuse Prevention	5800 West 10th Street Freeway Medical Center Suite 907 Little Rock, AR 72204	501-280-4515	501-280-4519
California Department of Alcohol and Drug Programs	1700 K Street Sacramento, CA 95814-4037	800-879-2772	916-323-1270
Colorado Department of Human Services	4055 S. Lowell Blvd. Denver, CO 80236-3120	303-866-7480	303-866-7481
Connecticut Department of Mental Health and Addiction Services	410 Capitol Avenue 4th Floor Hartford, CT 06134	860-418-6838	860-418-6792

STATE DEPARTMENT	ADDRESS	TELEPHONE	FACSIMILE
Delaware Division of Substance Abuse and Mental Health	1901 North DuPont Highway, First Floor New Castle, DE 19720	302-255-9399	302-255-4428
District of Columbia Department of Health	825 N. Capitol Street NE Suite 3132 Washington, DC 20002	202-442-9152	202-442-4827
Florida Substance Abuse Program Office	1317 Winewood Boulevard Building 6, Room 334 Tallahassee, FL 32399-0700	850-487-2920	850-487-2239
Georgia Department of Mental Health and Substance Abuse	Two Peachtree Street NW Suite 23-204 Atlanta, GA 30303-3171	404-657-2135	404-657-2160
Hawaii Department of Health	Kakuhihewa Bldg. 601 Kamokila Blvd. Rm 360 Kapolei, HI 96707	808-692-7506	808-692-7521
Idaho Department of Health & Welfare	450 West State Street 5th Fl, P.O. Box 83720, Boise, ID 83720-0036	208-334-5935	208-332-7305
Illinois Office of Alcoholism and Substance Abuse	100 West Randolph Suite 5-600 Chicago, IL 60601	312-814-3840	312-814-2419
Indiana Division of Mental Health and Addiction	402 West Washington Street, Room W353 Indianapolis, IN 46204-2739	317-232-7800	317-233-3472
Iowa Department of Public Health	Lucas State Office Building, 4th Floor 321 East 12th Street Des Moines IA 50319-0075	515-281-4417	515-281-4535
Kansas Department of Social Rehabilitation	915 Harrison Street Topeka, KS 66612	785-291-3326	785-296-7275

STATE DEPARTMENT	ADDRESS	TELEPHONE	FACSIMILE
Kentucky Department of Mental Health Services	100 Fair Oaks Lane, 4E-D Frankfort, KY 40621	502-564-2880	502-564-7152
Louisiana Department of Health and Hospitals	1201 Capitol Access Road 4th Fl. Baton Rouge, LA 70821-2790	225-342-6717	225-342-3875
Maine Office of Substance Abuse	AMHI Complex, Marquardt Bldg., 3rd Floor Augusta, ME 04333-0159	207-287-2595	207-287-4334
Maryland Department of Health and Mental Hygiene	55 Wade Avenue Catonsville, MD 21228	410-402-8600	410-402-8601
Massachusetts Bureau of Substance Abuse Services	250 Washington Street 3rd Fl. Boston, MA 02108-4619	617-624-5111	617-624-5185
Michigan Bureau of Mental Health and Substance Abuse Services	320 South Walnut, 6th Fl. Lansing, MI 48909	517-241-2596	517-241-2345
Minnesota Department of Human Services	444 Lafayette Road Saint Paul, MN 55155-3823	651-582-1832	651-582-1865
Mississippi Department of Mental Health,	Robert E Lee Office Building, 11th Fl. 239 North Lamar Street Jackson MS 39201	877-210-8513	601-359-6295
Missouri Division of Alcohol and Drug Abuse	1706 East Elm Street Jefferson City, MO 65102	573-751-4942	573-751-7814
Montana Addictive and Mental Disorders Division	555 Fuller Helena, MT 59620-2905	406-444-3964	406-444-9389

STATE DEPARTMENT	ADDRESS	TELEPHONE	FACSIMILE
Nebraska Substance Abuse and Addiction Services	P.O. Box 98925 Lincoln, NE 68509-8925	402-479-5583	402-479-5162
Nevada Bureau of Alcohol and Drug Abuse	505 E King Street, Rm 500 Carson City, NV 89701	775-684-4190	775-684-4185
New Hampshire Division of Alcohol and Drug Abuse	105 Pleasant Street Concord, NH 03301	800-804-0909	603-271-6116
New Jersey Division of Addiction Services	120 S Stockton Street 3rd Floor Trenton, NJ 08625-0362	609-292-5760	609-292-3816
New Mexico Department of Health	1190 Saint Francis Drive Harold Runnels Bldg. Santa Fe, NM 87502	505-827-2601	505-827-0097
New York Office of Alcoholism and Substance Abuse Services	1450 Western Avenue Albany, NY 12203-3526	518-473-3460	518-457-5474
North Carolina Substance Abuse Services	325 North Salisbury St. Suite 1156-P Raleigh, NC 27699-3007	919-733-4670	919-733-9455
North Dakota Division of Mental Health and Substance Abuse Services	600 South 2nd St. Suite 1E Bismarck, ND 58504-5729	701-328-8920	701-328-8969
Ohio Department of Alcohol and Drug Addiction Services	280 North High Street 12th Floor Columbus, OH 43215-2537	614-466-3445	614-752-8645
Oklahoma Substance Abuse Program	1200 NE 13th, 2nd Floor Oklahoma City OK 73152-3277	405-522-3877	405-522-0637

STATE DEPARTMENT	ADDRESS	TELEPHONE	FACSIMILE
Oregon Office of Mental Health and Addiction Services	500 Summer Street NE Salem, OR 97301-1118	503-945-5763	503-378-8467
Pennsylvania Bureau of Drug and Alcohol . Programs	02 Kline Plaza, Suite B Harrisburg, PA 17104	717-783-8200	717-787-6285
Rhode Island Division of Behavioral Health	14 Harrington Road Cranston, RI 02920	401-462-4680	401-462-6078
South Carolina Department of Alcohol and Other Drug Abuse Services	101 Business Park Blvd. Columbia, SC 29203-9498	803-896-5555	803-896-5557
South Dakota Division of Alcohol and Drug Abuse	500 East Capitol Pierre, SD 57501-5070	605-773-3123	605-773-7076
Tennessee Bureau of Alcohol and Drug Abuse Services	425 5th Avenue North Nashville, TN 37247-4401	615-741-1921	615-532-2419
Texas Commission on Alcohol and Drug Abuse	9001 North IH 35 Suite 105 Austin TX 78708-0529	512-349-6600	512-837-0998
Utah Division of Substance Abuse and Mental Health	120 North 200 West 2nd Floor, Room 201 Salt Lake City, UT 84103	801-538-3939	801-538-4696
Vermont Division of Alcohol and Drug Abuse Programs	108 Cherry Street Burlington, VT 05402	802-651-1550	802-651-1573
Virginia Office of Substance Abuse Services	1220 Bank Street Richmond, VA 23218-1797	804-786-3906	804-786-4320

STATE DEPARTMENT	ADDRESS	TELEPHONE	FACSIMILE
Washington Division of Alcohol and Substance Abuse	612 Woodland Sq. Olympia, WA 98504-5330	877-301-4557	360-438-8078
West Virginia Department of Health and Human Services	350 Capitol Street Rm. 350 Charleston, WV 25301-3702	304-558-2276	304-558-1008
Wisconsin Bureau of Substance Abuse Services	1 West Wilson Street Madison, WI 53707-7851	608-266-2717	608-266-1533
Wyoming Substance Abuse Division	2424 Pioneer Avenue Suite 306 Cheyenne, WY 82002-0480	307-777-3358	307-777-7006[1]

---

1   Source: U.S. Department of Health and Human Services, Substance Abuse and Mental Health Services Administration.

APPENDIX 2:
TABLE OF FREQUENTLY USED ILLEGAL DRUGS

DRUG NAME	DESCRIPTION	USE	EFFECT
MARIJUANA	Marijuana—also known as "cannabis"—is the most frequently used illegal drug in the U.S.	Marijuana is a green, brown or greyish mixture of dried, shredded leaves, stems; seeds and flowers of the hemp plant. Marijuana is rolled loose into a cigarette—commonly referred to as a "joint," smoked in a pipe, or mixed into foods	Marijuana's effect depends on potency of THC (tetrahydrocannabinol), the main active ingredient. Includes impairment of short-term memory, concentration and motor skills; possible long-term physical and psychological dependence and/or slowed reaction time, impaired coordination and decrease attention span.

DRUG NAME	DESCRIPTION	USE	EFFECT
COCAINE/CRACK	Cocaine is a white powder that is derived from the South American coca plant. Crack is a chemically altered smokeable form of cocaine in the form of pellets or crystalline rocks	Cocaine can either be snorted or injected and produces a high lasting about 20 minutes. Crack cocaine is smoked with effects lasting about 12 minutes	Both cocaine and crack are highly addictive. Cocaine can increase blood pressure, heart and breathing rates and body temperature and lead to heart attacks, strokes or respiratory failure. Cocaine also lowers the body's resistance and ability to fight infection. Cocaine can also cause violent or paranoid behavior, hallucinations, confusion, anxiety or depression. Once the drug leaves the brain the user experiences depression, irritability, and fatigue.
HEROIN	Heroin is a white-to-brownish tar-like substance or powder derived from morphine	Heroin can be injected, smoked or inhaled, and heroin users quickly adopt a tolerance for the drug and must use increasing amounts to get the same effects	Heroin is highly addictive and can cause slowed and slurred speech, respiratory depression, an impaired immune system, HIV infection from injection, decreased sexual pleasure, sedation proceeding to coma, reduced appetite, irregular heart rate or blood pressure, or death.

DRUG NAME	DESCRIPTION	USE	EFFECT
METHAMPHETAMINE	Methamphetamine—also known as "meth," "speed" or "crank" is a stimulant drug that affects the central nervous system, and is found in a pill or powdered form	Methamphetamine can be swallowed, snorted, injected or smoked, and users quickly adopt a tolerance for the drug and must use increasing amounts to get the same effects	Methamphetamine can increase heart rate and blood pressure, and cause insomnia, increased physical activity or produce symptoms of paranoia.
LSD	LSD—also known as "acid, "—is a hallucinogen, i.e., a potent mood-changing drug, which is found in tablets, capsules or liquid form	LSD can be swallowed or licked off paper	LSD effects may include panic, confusion, suspicion, and anxiety. Users can also experience flashbacks after they have stopped using the drug.
ECSTASY	Ecstasy is a synthetic or "designer" drug derived from speed and methamphetamine, and can be found in capsule, tablet, powder or liquid forms	Ecstasy can be swallowed, snorted, injected or smoked	Ecstasy acts simultaneously as a stimulant and a hallucinogen, and produces hallucinogenic effects. It can affect mood, sleeping and eating habits, thinking processes, aggressive behavior, sexual function, and sensitivity to pain. It can also increase blood pressure and heart rate, and users risk exhaustion and dehydration from a combination of taking the drug and exertion, such as non-stop dancing, leading to death from heat stroke.

DRUG NAME	DESCRIPTION	USE	EFFECT
INHALANTS	Inhalants are readily available substances such as paint, glue, typewriter correction fluid, felt tip markers, spray paint, air freshener, and butane	Inhalants are sniffed or "huffed" to give the user an immediate high	Sniffing inhalants can cause sudden death, suffocation, and hallucinations.
STEROIDS	Steroids are synthetic compounds related to the male sex hormone testosterone which are available in tablet or liquid form	Steroids are swallowed or injected directly into muscles, and are often used illegally by body-builders, long-distance runners and other athletes who claim that steroids give them a competitive advantage or improve their physical appearance	Steroids may contribute to increases in body weight and muscular strength when used in combination with a program of muscle-building exercise and diet, and users can be affected by more than 70 side effects including psychological as well as physical reactions, the most serious of which affect the liver, cardiovascular and reproductive systems. Steroids can also produce aggressive behavior and interfere with bone growth in young adults.

DRUG NAME	DESCRIPTION	USE	EFFECT
ALCOHOL	Alcohol is the most widely tried drug among teenagers and is the most commonly used and widely abused drug in the country. It is found in beers, wines and hard liquors	Alcohol is swallowed, absorbed by the stomach, enters the bloodstream, and goes to all tissues	Alcohol's effects vary depending on the user's size, weight, age and sex, as well as the amount of food and alcohol consumed. Alcohol can act as a disinhibitor and also produce dizziness, slurred speech, nausea and vomiting. Even at low to moderate doses alcohol can significantly impair judgment and coordination, increase aggressiveness, and produce hangovers with effects such as headache, nausea, thirst, dizziness and fatigue. Long-term effects of large quantities of alcohol can lead to permanent damage to vital organs such as the brain and liver.
TOBACCO	Tobacco can be found in cigarettes, cigars, pipes, tobacco and smokeless tobacco and nicotine is the drug in tobacco that causes addiction	Tobacco is usually smoked although it can be chewed	Smoking is a major cause of stroke and the third-leading cause of death in the United States. Smoking-related heart disease result in 170,000 deaths annually.[1]

1   Source: The National Center on Addiction and Substance Abuse at Columbia University.

APPENDIX 3:
ANNUAL MARIJUANA USAGE AMONG
COLLEGE STUDENTS (1980-2000)

YEAR	ANNUAL USAGE
1989-1991	26.4%
1990-1992	24.2%
1991-1993	24.5%
1992-1994	27.7%
1995	29.8%
1996	32.2%
1997	32.3%
1998	32.4%
1999	32.5%
2000	33.6%

APPENDIX 4:
SAMPLE COLLEGE DRUG AND
ALCOHOL POLICY

DRUGS AND ALCOHOL

College expects its students and employees to maintain an environment that is safe and healthy. The unlawful possession, use, or distribution of illicit drugs and alcohol by students and employees on College property or as a part of any College activity are violations of University rules as well as the law.

Possession, use, or distribution of certain non-prescription drugs, including marijuana, amphetamines, heroin, cocaine, and non-prescription synthetics; procurement or distribution of alcohol by anyone under 21 years of age; and provision of alcohol to anyone under 21 years of age are violations of the law and of College policy.

The University holds its students and employees responsible for the consequences of their decisions to use or distribute illicit drugs or to serve or consume alcohol.

HEALTH CONCERNS

The use of illicit drugs and the misuse of alcohol are potentially harmful to health. In particular, synthetically produced drugs often have unpredictable emotional and physical side effects that constitute an extreme health hazard. Students should also weigh the seriousness of potential loss of function that may come from ingesting illicit drugs or too much alcohol.

Because of the considerable hazards involved in drug and alcohol use, administrative, medical, and psychiatric help for students having alcohol or other drug problems are available on a confidential basis from the University Health Services Bureau. Any member of the University may make use of the Health Services on an emergency basis, day and night.

ILLEGAL ACTS

Careful note should be taken that the University is not, and cannot be considered as, a protector or sanctuary from the existing laws of the city, state, or federal government. State law prohibits the sale, delivery, or furnishing of alcohol to persons under the age of 21.

In addition, a social host may under certain circumstances be held liable for injuries caused by a guest who, having consumed alcohol on the host's premises, does harm to himself or herself or to a third party. If the guest is a minor (i.e. under 21) and the host knew or reasonably should have known that he or she was furnishing alcohol to a minor, the host will be held responsible for injuries or damage to the minor or to third parties caused by the minor's alcohol-influenced actions.

Further, even if the guest was not a minor, a social host will be liable for injuries to third parties if the host knew or should have known that the guest was intoxicated, but nevertheless gave him or her, or permitted him or her to take, an alcoholic drink.

Students are reminded that there are heavy penalties, including imprisonment, for possession or distribution of illicit drugs and for selling or delivering alcohol to, or procuring alcohol for, anyone under 21. There are also serious penalties for anyone under the age of 21 who purchases, attempts to purchase, or arranges to procure alcoholic beverages or to misrepresent his or her age or falsify his or her identification with the intent of purchasing alcohol, as well as for anyone, regardless of age, who operates a motor vehicle under the influence of alcohol or drugs, or with an open container of alcohol. In addition, City ordinances prohibit consumption of alcohol on public property or on property open to the public.

DISCIPLINARY ACTION

The University requires all students to become familiar with the information on drugs and alcohol distributed at registration each year. In addition, the General Counsel to the University has prepared a pamphlet on drug and alcohol laws that is available in the administrative offices. When cases involving drugs and alcohol come to the attention of the College, it may take disciplinary action, including requirement to withdraw.

Officers of the College may initially respond to the use of illicit drugs, underage possession or consumption of alcohol, serving alcohol to underage individuals, and overconsumption of alcohol with a warning and/or referral to health or counseling services. A pattern of behavior in violation of these rules will lead to warning by the House Master or Dean of Freshmen, admonition by the Administrative Board, probation, or requirement to withdraw.

The Administrative Board will take serious action, ordinarily probation or requirement to withdraw, in any case involving the possession in quantity or the sale or distribution of drugs, or when cases of drug and alcohol use involve danger to individuals or to the community at large. The Administrative Board will also take action in cases in which a student falsifies his or her identification with the intent of obtaining alcohol.

APPENDIX 5:
STATE ENFORCING THE UNDERAGE DRINKING LAWS (EUDL) PROGRAM COORDINATORS

STATE	AGENCY	ADDRESS	TELEPHONE
Alabama	Department of Economic and Community Affairs	401 Adams Avenue P.O. Box 5690 Montgomery, AL 36103-5690	334-242-5812
Alaska	Department of Health and Human Services	Division of Juvenile Justice P.O. Box 110635 Juneau, AK 99811-0635	907-465-2116
Arkansas	Department of Finance and Administration, Alcohol Beverage Control Enforcement	1509 West 7th Street P.O. Box 3278 Little Rock, AR 72203	N/A
Arizona	Governor's Office of Community and Highway Safety (GOCHS)	3030 North Central #1550 Phoenix, AZ 85012	N/A
California	Office of Traffic Safety	7000 Franklin Blvd. Suite 440 Sacramento, CA 95823-1820	N/A
Colorado	Department of Transportation	4201 East Arkansas Avenue Denver, CO 80222	303-757-9465
Connecticut	Office of Policy and Management, Policy Development and Planning Division	450 Capitol Avenue-MD#52CPD Hartford, CT 06106	N/A

STATE	AGENCY	ADDRESS	TELEPHONE
District of Columbia	Justice Grants Administration	441 4th Street NW 11th Floor Washington, DC 20001	N/A
Delaware	Department of Highway Safety, Office of Highway Safety Public Safety Building	303 Transportation Circle, Suite 201 Dover, DE 19903	302-744-2748
Florida	Department of Business and Professional Regulation	Northwood Center 1940 North Monroe Street Tallahassee, FL 32399-1020	N/A
Georgia	Atlanta Coordinating Counsel	10 Park Place South Suite 410 Atlanta, GA 30303	404-463-0240
Idaho	Juvenile Justice Commission, Idaho Department of Juvenile Corrections	P.O. Box 83720 Boise, ID 83720-0285	N/A
Hawaii	Department of Human Services, Office of Youth Services	1481 South King Street Honolulu, HI 96814	N/A
Iowa	Department of Human Rights, Division of Criminal and Juvenile Justice Planning	Lucas State Office Building Des Moines, IA 50319	N/A
Indiana	Criminal Justice Institute	One North Capitol Avenue, Suite 1000 Indianapolis, IN 46204-1233	N/A
Illinois	Department Human Services	160 North LaSalle 7th Floor Chicago, IL 60601	N/A
Louisiana	Office of Alcohol and Tobacco Control	1885 Wooddale Boulevard, 6th Floor P.O. Box 66404 Baton Rouge, LA 70806	N/A

STATE	AGENCY	ADDRESS	TELEPHONE
Kansas	Department of Transportation, Bureau of Traffic Safety	217 South East 4th Street Topeka, KS 66603-3504	N/A
Kentucky	State Police	403 Wapping Street Bush Building, Suite 103 Frankfort, KY 40601	502-564-6700
Maine	Office of Substance Abuse	AMHI Complex Marquardt Building 3rd Floor 159 State House Station Augusta, ME 04333-0159	N/A
Massachusetts	Executive Office of Public Safety, Governor's Highway Safety Bureau	10 Park Plaza Suite 5220 Boston, MA 02116-3933	N/A
Maryland	Governor's Office of Crime Control and Prevention	300 East Joppa Road Suite 1105 Towson, MD 21286-3016	410-321-3521
Michigan	State Police, Office of Highway Safety Planning	400 Collins Road P.O. Box 30633 Lansing, MI 48909-8133	N/A
Minnesota	Department of Public Safety, Office of Traffic Safety	444 Cedar Street Suite 150 St. Paul, MN 55101-5150	N/A
North Carolina	Department of Health and Human Services	2001 Mail Service Center Raleigh, NC 27699-2001	N/A
Mississippi	Division of Public Safety Planning, Office of Highway Safety	3750 I-55 North Frontage Road Jackson, MS 39211	601-987-4184
Montana	Board of Crime Control	3075 North Montana Avenue Helena, MT 59601	406-444-2056

STATE	AGENCY	ADDRESS	TELEPHONE
North Dakota	Department of Human Services, Division of Mental Health and Substance Abuse	600 South 2nd Street Suite #1E Bismarck, ND 58504-5729	N/A
Nebraska	Office of Highway Safety, Department of Motor Vehicles	301 Centennial Mall South P.O. Box 94612 Lincoln, NE 68509	N/A
New Hampshire	Department of Justice	33 Capitol Street Concord, NH 03301	N/A
Nevada	Department of Human Resources	400 West King Street Suite 230 Carson City, NV 89703	N/A
New York	State Office of Alcoholism & Substance Abuse Services	1450 Western Avenue Albany, NY 12203-3526	N/A
New Jersey	Division of Alcohol Beverage Control	P.O. Box 087 Trenton, NJ 08625	N/A
New Mexico	Children, Youth, and Families Department	P.O. Drawer 5160 Santa Fe, NM 87502-5160	505-827-6325
Ohio	Department of Alcohol and Drug Addiction Services Two Nationwide Plaza	280 North High Street 12th Floor Columbus, OH 43215-2537	N/A
Pennsylvania	State Police, Bureau of Liquor Control Enforcement	3655 Vartan Way Harrisburg, PA 17110	N/A
Oklahoma	Department of Public Safety, Highway Safety Office	3223 North Lincoln Blvd. Oklahoma City, OK 73105	N/A
Oregon	Office of Alcohol and Drug Abuse Programs	500 Summer Street NE Salem, OR 97310-1016	N/A

STATE	AGENCY	ADDRESS	TELEPHONE
Rhode Island	Department of Mental Health Retardation and Hospitals, Division of Substance Abuse	14 Harrington Road/Barry Hall 3rd Floor Cranston, RI 02920	N/A
South Carolina	Department of Alcohol and Other Abuse Services	101 Business Park Boulevard Columbia, SC 29203-9498	803-896-1175
South Dakota	Office of Highway Safety, Department of Commerce and Regulation	118 West Capitol Avenue Pierre, SD 57501-2000	605-773-4088
Tennessee	Department of Children's Services, Cordell Hull Building	436 Sixth Avenue North 8th Floor Nashville, TN 37248-1290	615-741-5278
Virginia	Alcoholic Beverage Control Education and Training	2901 Hermitage Road Richmond VA 23220	N/A
Texas	Office of the Governor, Criminal Justice Division	P.O. Box 12428 Austin, TX 78711	N/A
Utah	Highway Safety Office	5263 Commerce Drive Suite 202 Salt Lake City, UT 84107	N/A
Washington	Department of Social and Health Services	P.O. Box 45330 Olympia, WA 98504-5330	360-438-8200
Vermont	Department of Health, Office of Alcohol and Drug Abuse Programs	P.O. Box 70 Burlington VT 05402-0070	N/A
Wisconsin	Department of Transportation, Bureau of Transportation Safety	4802 Sheboygan Avenue Madison, WI 53705	N/A

STATE	AGENCY	ADDRESS	TELEPHONE
West Virginia	Division of Criminal Justice Services	1204 Kanawha Boulevard East Charleston, WV 25301	304-558-8814
Wyoming	Department of Health, Substance Abuse	2424 Pioneer Avenue Suite 306 Cheyenne WY 82002	307-777-6885

APPENDIX 6:
STATE ILLEGAL PER SE BLOOD ALCOHOL CONCENTRATION (BAC) LEVELS— YOUNG DRIVERS (UNDER 21)

STATE	ILLEGAL PER SE BAC LEVEL	SEE FOOTNOTE
ALABAMA	0.02	
ALASKA	0.00	
ARIZONA	0.00	
ARKANSAS	0.02	
CALIFORNIA	0.01	
COLORADO	0.02	
CONNECTICUT	0.02	
DELAWARE	0.02	1
DISTRICT OF COLUMBIA	0.02	
FLORIDA	0.02	
GEORGIA	0.02	
HAWAII	0.02	
IDAHO	0.02	
ILLINOIS	0.00	
INDIANA	0.02	
IOWA	0.02	
KANSAS	0.02	

STATE	ILLEGAL PER SE BAC LEVEL	SEE FOOTNOTE
KENTUCKY	0.02	
LOUISIANA	0.02	
MAINE	0.00	
MARYLAND	0.02	
MASSACHUSETTS	0.02	
MICHIGAN	0.02	
MINNESOTA	0.00	
MISSISSIPPI	0.08	
MISSOURI	0.02	
MONTANA	0.02	
NEBRASKA	0.02	
NEVADA	0.02	
NEW HAMPSHIRE	0.02	
NEW JERSEY	0.01	
NEW MEXICO	0.02	
NEW YORK	0.02	
NORTH CAROLINA	0.00	
NORTH DAKOTA	0.02	
OHIO	0.02	
OKLAHOMA	0.00	
OREGON	0.00	
PENNSYLVANIA	0.02	
RHODE ISLAND	0.02	
SOUTH CAROLINA	N/A	
SOUTH DAKOTA	N/A	
TENNESSEE	0.02	
TEXAS	0.00	
UTAH	0.00	
VERMONT	0.02	

STATE	ILLEGAL PER SE BAC LEVEL	SEE FOOTNOTE
VIRGINIA	0.02	
WASHINGTON	0.02	
WEST VIRGINIA	0.02	
WISCONSIN	0.02	2
WYOMING	N/A	

1. *In Delaware, the 0.02 percent BAC law for young drivers isn't a per se law.*

2. *The Wisconsin statute applies to drivers under the age of 19.*[1]

1   Source: Insurance Institute for Highway Safety.

APPENDIX 7:
SELECTED IMPLIED CONSENT PROVISIONS OF THE UNIFORM VEHICLE CODE FOR DRIVERS UNDER AGE 21

SECTION 6-208(b). Any person under age (21) who drives or is in actual physical control of any vehicle upon the highways of this State shall be deemed to have given consent, subject to the provisions of §11-903, to a test or tests of such person's blood, breath, or urine for the purpose of determining such person's alcohol concentration or the presence of other drugs.

SECTION 6-208(d). A person under age (21) requested to submit to a test as provided above shall be warned by the law enforcement officer requesting the test that a refusal to submit to the test will result in revocation of such person's license to operate a vehicle for (six months) (one year). Following this warning, if a person under arrest refuses upon the request of a law enforcement officer to submit to a test designated by the law enforcement agency as provided in paragraph (b) of this section, none shall be given.

SECTION 6-208(e). If the person under the age (21) refuses testing or submits to a test which discloses an alcohol concentration of any measurable and detectable amount under this section, the law enforcement officer shall submit a sworn report to the department, certifying that the test was requested pursuant to subsection (b) and that the person refused to submit to testing or submitted to a test which disclosed an alcohol concentration of any measurable and detectable amount.

SECTION 6-208(f). Upon receipt of the sworn report of a law enforcement officer submitted under subsection (e), the department shall revoke the driver's license of the person for the periods specified in §6-214.

APPENDIX 8:
RESOURCE DIRECTORY OF STATES PUBLISHING YOUTH TOBACCO SURVEY REPORTS

STATE	AGENCY	TELEPHONE	WEBSITE AVAILABILITY OF REPORT
Arkansas	Arkansas Department of Health	(501) 661-2785	No
Florida	Florida Department of Health	(850) 245-4401	www.state.fl.us/tobacco
Georgia	Georgia Department of Human Resources	(404) 657-6645	No
Kansas	Kansas Department of Health and Environment	(785) 296-1207	No
Mississippi	Mississippi State Department of Health	(601) 576-7428	www.msdh.state.ms.us/tobacco
Missouri	Missouri Department of Health	(573) 522-2800	www.health.state.mo.us/SmokingAndTobacco

STATE	AGENCY	TELEPHONE	WEBSITE AVAILABILITY OF REPORT
Nebraska	Department of Health and Human Services Regulation and Licensure	(402) 471-0920	No
New Jersey	New Jersey Department of Health and Senior Services	(609) 292-4414	www.state.nj.us/health/as/smoking.htm
North Carolina	North Carolina Department of Health and Human Services	(919) 733-1881	www.communityhealth.dhhs.state.nc.us/tobacco/Survey/survey.htm
Oklahoma	Oklahoma State Department of Health	(405) 271-3619	www.health.state.ok.us/PROGRAM/tobac/index.html
South Dakota	South Dakota Department of Human Services	(605) 773-3123	No
Tennessee	Tennessee Department of Health	(615) 741-0380	No
Texas	Texas Department of Health	(512) 458-7200	www.tdh.state.tx.us/otpc [1]

Source: Centers for Disease Control and Prevention (CDC).

1

APPENDIX 9:
ANABOLIC STEROID USE BY STUDENTS (2000)

USAGE RATE	8TH GRADERS	10TH GRADERS	12TH GRADERS
Lifetime	3.0%	3.5%	2.5%
Used in Past Year	1.7	2.2	1.7
Used in Past Month	0.8	1.0	0.8

1. "Lifetime" refers to use at least once during a respondent's lifetime.

2. "Past year" refers to an individual's drug use at least once during the year preceding their response to the survey.

3. "Past month" refers to an individual's drug use at least once during the month preceding their response to the survey. [1]

---

1   Source: National Institute on Drug Abuse, 2000 Monitoring the Future Study.

APPENDIX 10:
ANNUAL MARIJUANA USAGE AMONG
COLLEGE ATHLETES (1985-2001)

YEAR	ANNUAL USAGE
1985	35.3%
1989	27.5%
1993	21.4%
1997	28.4%
2001	27.3% [1]

---

1   Source: The National Collegiate Athletic Association (NCAA).

GLOSSARY

ACF—Administration for Children and Families.

ADAM—Arrestee Drug Abuse Monitoring System, formerly known as the Drug Use Forecasting (DUF) program.

Adjudicatory Hearing—The process by which it is determined whether the allegations in a complaint can be proven, and, if so, whether they fall within the jurisdictional categories of the juvenile court.

Administrative License Revocation—A law which gives state officials the authority to suspend administratively the license of any driver who fails, or refuses to take, a BAC test.

AIDS—Acquired Immune Deficiency Syndrome.

Alcohol Per Se Laws—Laws which make it illegal to drive with an alcohol concentration measured at or above a certain level.

ATF—Bureau of Alcohol, Tobacco and Firearms.

ATS—Amphetamine-Type Stimulants.

Binge Drinker—Youth admits having 5 or more drinks on the same occasion at last once in the 30 days prior to a survey.

BJA—Bureau of Justice Assistance, part of the U.S. Department of Justice.

BJS—Bureau of Justice Statistics, part of the U.S. Department of Justice.

Blood Alcohol Concentration (BAC)—The amount of alcohol in the bloodstream, measured in percentages.

BOP—Bureau of Prisons, part of the U.S. Department of Justice.

CADCA—Community Anti-Drug Coalitions of America.

Capacity—Capacity is the legal qualification concerning the ability of one to understand the nature and effects of one's acts.

CAPTs—Centers for the Application of Prevention Technologies.

CASA—Center on Addiction and Substance Abuse, a research organization based at Columbia University.

CDC—Centers for Disease Control and Prevention.

CICAD—Inter-American Drug Abuse Control Commission, a body of the Organization of American States.

Compliance Checks—Typically involves underage individuals making tobacco purchase attempts under the control and guidance of law enforcement in order to check retailer compliance with minimum age purchase laws.

COPS—Community Oriented Policing Services, a program of the Department of Justice.

Craving—As it relates to alcohol, craving is a strong need, or urge, to drink alcohol.

CSAP—Center for Substance Abuse Prevention, a component of SAMHSA, an operating division within the Department of Health and Human Services.

CSAT—Center for Substance Abuse Treatment, a component of SAMHSA, an operating division within the Department of Health and Human Services.

CTAC—Counter-Drug Technology Assessment Center.

CTN—National Drug Abuse Treatment Clinical Trials Network.

Current Drinker—Youth admits having at least one drink in the 30 days prior to a survey.

D.A.R.E.—Drug Abuse Resistance Education.

DATOS—Drug Abuse Treatment Outcome Study, run by the National Institute on Drug Abuse.

DAWN—Drug Abuse Warning Network, a SAMHSA-funded program which monitors drug abuse among persons admitted at hospital emergency rooms.

DEA—Drug Enforcement Administration, part of the Department of Justice.

DEFY—Drug Education for Youth.

Delinquent—An infant of not more than a specified age who has violated criminal laws or engages in disobedient, indecent or immoral conduct, and is in need of treatment, rehabilitation, or supervision.

DENS—Drug Evaluation Network System.

DFS3—Drug-Free Schools State Supplement.

DOD—U.S. Department of Defense.

DOJ—U.S. Department of Justice.

DOT—U.S. Department of Transportation.

Driver's License—Any license to operate a motor vehicle issued under the laws of a particular state.

Drug Episode—An emergency department visit that was related to the use of an illegal drug, or the non-medical use of a legal drug for patients aged six years and older.

DUF—Drug Use Forecasting program, now known as ADAM.

FAS—Fetal Alcohol Syndrome.

FDA—Food and Drug Administration, part of the Department of Health and Human Services.

Felony—A crime of a graver or more serious nature than those designated as misdemeanors. Under federal law, and many state statutes, any offense punishable by death or imprisonment for a term exceeding one year.

GBL—Gamma-Butyrolactone.

GCIP—General Counterdrug Intelligence Plan.

GHB—Gamma-Hydroxybutyrate.

Hallucinogens—Natural and man-made drugs which affect the mind, causing distortions in physical senses and mental reactions.

Hcl—Cocaine Hydrochloride.

Heavy Drinker—Youth admits having 5 or more drinks on the same occasion on at least 5 different days in the month prior to a survey.

HHS—U.S. Department of Health and Human Services.

HIDTA—High Intensity Drug Trafficking Area, a counter-drug initiative overseen by the Office of National Drug Control Policy.

HIV—Human Immunodeficiency Virus.

IDU—Injection Drug User.

Ignition Interlock—A device which has a breath tester that drivers blow into to measure their blood alcohol level and which, if alcohol is detected, prevent the vehicle from starting.

Illegal—Against the law.

Illegal Per Se—Illegal in and of itself.

Inhalants—Chemicals which emit fumes or vapors which, when inhaled, produce symptoms similar to intoxication.

IOM—Institute of Medicine, part of the National Academy of Science.

Juvenile Court—A court which has special jurisdiction, of a parental nature, over delinquent, dependent and neglected children.

Keg Registration Laws—Laws which require beer kegs and other large alcohol containers to be tagged and for the purchasers name and the address where the beverage is to be served to be recorded.

LAAM—Levo-Alph-Acetyl-Methadol.

Loss of control—As it relates to alcohol, loss of control means not being able to stop drinking once drinking has begun.

LSD—Lysergic acid diethylamide, a hallucinogen.

MDMA—3,4-methylenedioxymethamphetamine, an illegally produced stimulant that has hallucinogenic properties.

NAADAC—National Association of Alcoholism and Drug Abuse Counselors.

Narcotics—Generic term for any drug which dulls the senses or induces sleep and which commonly becomes addictive after prolonged use.

NASADAD—National Association of State Alcohol and Drug Abuse Directors.

NATA—Narcotic Addict Treatment Act.

NCHS—National Center for Health Statistics.

NDATUS—National Drug and Alcoholism Treatment Unit Survey.

NDIC—National Drug Intelligence Center.

NHSDA—National Household Survey of Drug Abuse, the most comprehensive of the many national surveys of drug abuse, funded by SAMHSA.

NHTSA—National Highway Traffic Safety Administration, part of the Department of Transportation.

NIAAA—National Institute on Alcohol Abuse and Alcoholism, one of the National Institutes of Health and part of the Department of Health and Human Services.

NIDA—National Institute on Drug Abuse, one of the National Institutes of Health and part of the Department of Health and Human Services.

NIH—National Institutes of Health, part of the Department of Health and Human Services.

NIJ—National Institute of Justice, part of the Department of Justice.

NIMH—National Institute of Mental Health.

OCDETF—Organized Crime Drug Enforcement Task Force, a program of the Department of Justice.

OJJDP—Office of Juvenile Justice and Delinquency Prevention, part of the Department of Justice.

OJP—Office of Justice Programs, part of the Department of Justice.

ONDCP—Office of National Drug Control Policy.

Open Container Laws—Laws which prohibit the possession of any open alcoholic beverage container and the consumption of any alcoholic beverage in the passenger area of a motor vehicle.

PCP—Phencyclidine, a clandestinely manufactured hallucinogen.

PDFA—Partnership for a Drug-Free America, a private organization that promotes private-sector involvement in the creation of anti-drug messages.

Peers—Those who are a man's equals in rank and station.

Physical dependence—As it relates to alcohol, physical dependence results in withdrawal symptoms, such as nausea, sweating, shakiness, and anxiety after stopping drinking.

PRIDE—Parent's Resource Institute for Drug Education.

PSA—Public Service Announcement.

Rave—A rave is a dance party, characterized by loud, rapid-tempo "techno" music, light shows, smoke or fog, and pyrotechnics.

Responsible Beverage Service—Refers to an educational training program that trains and alcohol servers and alcohol outlet managers how to avoid the illegal sale of alcohol to underage youth or intoxicated patrons.

Revocation—The termination by formal action of a person's license or privilege to operate a motor vehicle on the highways, which terminated license or privilege shall not be subject to renewal or restoration except that an application for a new license may be presented and acted upon by the department after the expiration of the applicable period of time.

RSAT—Residential Substance Abuse Treatment.

SAID—Substance Abuse Information Database.

SAMHSA—Substance Abuse and Mental Health Services Administration, an operating division within the Department of Health and Human Services.

SAPT—Substance Abuse Prevention and Treatment.

SDFSCA—Safe and Drug Free Schools and Communities Act.

SDFSP—Safe and Drug-Free Schools and Communities Program.

Single Parent Family—A family in which one parent remains the primary caretaker of the children, and the children maintain little or not contact with the other parent.

STD—Sexually Transmitted Disease.

Suicide—The deliberate termination of one's existence.

Suspension—The temporary withdrawal by formal action of a person's license or privilege to operate a motor vehicle on the public highways, which temporary withdrawal shall be for a period specifically designated.

THC—Tetrahydrocannabinol, the psychoactive substance in marijuana.

Tolerance—As it relates to alcohol, tolerance refers to the need to drink greater amounts of alcohol to get "high."

Truancy—Wilful and unjustified failure to attend school by one who is required to attend.

Underage Drinking—Underage drinking refers to any child, adolescent, or young person under the age of 21, who drinks alcohol.

XTC—A street name for MDMA.

YRBS—Youth Risk Behavior Survey.

Zero Tolerance Laws—Laws which make it illegal for drivers under age 21 to drive with any measurable amount of alcohol in their system regardless of the BAC limit for older drivers.

BIBLIOGRAPHY AND ADDITIONAL RESOURCES

Al-Anon Family Group Headquarters (Date Visited: May 2003) <http://www.al-anon.alateen.org/>.

Alcoholics Anonymous (Date Visited: May 2003) <http://www.aa.org/>.

Black's Law Dictionary, Fifth Edition. St. Paul, MN: West Publishing Company, 1979.

Centers for Disease Control and Prevention (Date Visited: May 2003) <http://www.cdc.gov/>.

Higher Education Center For Alcohol and Drug Prevention (Date Visited: May 2003) <http://www.edc.org/hec/>.

Insurance Institute for Highway Safety. (Date Visited: May 2003) <http://www.hwysafety.org/>.

Juvenile Justice Clearinghouse (JJC) (Date Visited: May 2003) <http://www.fsu.edu/~crimdo/jjclearinghouse/about.html/>.

Narcotics Anonymous (Date Visited: May 2003) <http://www.nanj.org/>.

The National Center on Addiction and Substance Abuse at Columbia University (CASA) (Date Visited: May 2003) <http://www.casacolumbia.org/>.

The National Clearinghouse for Alcohol and Drug Information (NCADI) (Date Visited: May 2003) <http://www.health.org/>.

The National Counsel on Alcoholism and Drug Dependence (NCADD) (Date Visited: May 2003) <http://www.ncadd.org/>.

The National Criminal Justice Reference Service (NCJRS) (Date Visited: May 2003) <http://www.ncjrs.org/>.

The National Drug Intelligence Center (NDIC) (Date Visited: May 2003) <http://ndicosa/>.

The National Highway Traffic and Safety Administration (NHTSA) (Date Visited: May 2003) <http://www.nhtsa.dot.gov/>.

The National Institute of Justice (NIJ) (Date Visited: May 2003) <http://www.ojp.usdoj.gov/nij/>.

The National Institute of Mental Health (NIMH) (Date Visited: May 2003) <http://www.nimh.nih.gov/>.

The National Institute on Alcohol Abuse and Alcoholism (NIAAA) (Date Visited: May 2003) <http://www.niaaa.nih.gov/>.

The National Institute on Drug Abuse (NIDA) (Date Visited: May 2003) <http://www.drugabuse.gov/>.

The Office of Justice Programs (OJP) (Date Visited: May 2003) <http://www.ojp.usdoj.gov/>.

The Office of Juvenile Justice and Delinquency Prevention (OJJDP) (Date Visited: May 2003) <http://ojjdp.ncjrs.org/>.

The Office of National Drug Control Policy (ONDCP) (Date Visited: May 2003) <http://www.whitehousedrugpolicy.gov/>.

Partnerships Against Violence Network (PAVNET) (Date Visited: May 2003) <http://www.pavnet.org/>.

The Prevention Decision Support System (DSS) (Date Visited: May 2003) <http://www.preventiondss.org/>.

Substance Abuse and Mental Health Services Administration (SAMHSA) (Date Visited: May 2003) <http://www.samhsa.gov/>.

The Substance Abuse Treatment Facility Locator (Date Visited: May 2003) <http://www.findtreatment.samhsa.gov/>.

The U.S. Consumer Product Safety Commission (Date Visited: May 2003) <http://www.cpsc.gov/>.

The U.S. Department of Education (Date Visited: May 2003) <http://www.ed.gov/>.

The U.S. Department of Education Safe and Drug-Free Schools Program (Date Visited: May 2003) <http://www.ed.gov/offices/OESE/SDFS/index.html>.

The U.S. Department of Health and Human Services (Date Visited: May 2003) <http://www.os.dhhs.gov/>.

The U.S. Department of Justice (Date Visited: May 2003) <http://www.usdoj.gov/>.

U.S. Department of Transportation, Underage Drinking Prevention Project (Date Visited: May 2003) <http://www.usdot.gov/>.

U.S. Drug Enforcement Administration (DEA) (Date Visited: May 2003) <http://www.usdoj.gov/dea>.

The U.S. Food and Drug Administration (FDA) (Date Visited: May 2003) <http://www.fda.gov/>.

The U.S. Office of Juvenile Justice and Delinquency Prevention (Date Visited: May 2003) <http://www.ojp.usdoj.gov/>.

The U.S. Office of National Drug Control Policy (Date Visited: May 2003) <http://www.ncjrs.org/>.